Composition
& Literature

Composition & Literature

Bridging the Gap

Edited by
Winifred Bryan Horner

The University of Chicago Press
Chicago & London

The University of Chicago Press, Chicago 60637
The University of Chicago Press, Ltd., London

Library of Congress Cataloging in Publication Data
Main entry under title:

Composition & literature.

   Includes index.
   1. English language—Rhetoric—Study and teaching—
Addresses, essays, lectures.   2. English literature—
Study and teaching (Higher)—Addresses, essays, lectures.
3. English philology—Study and teaching—Addresses,
essays, lectures.   I. Horner, Winifred Bryan.
II. Title: Composition and literature.
PE1404.C618   1983   808'.042'071173   83-3558
ISBN 0-226-35339-7 (cl.)
ISBN 0-226-35340-0 (pbk.)

Contents

v

Historical Introduction
Winifred Bryan Horner

This book comes out of a deep concern about the widening gulf between research and teaching in literature and research and teaching in composition. Such a separation represents a fracturing of the language discipline that is detrimental to work in both areas, as unproductive as it is unwarranted. In language and literature departments at most major universities, the study and teaching of literature are the serious business of departments of English and are supported by research funds and salaries and rewarded by promotion and tenure. The study and teaching of composition, on the other hand, are often considered peripheral.

The plan for the book was conceived after the meeting of the executive committee of the Teaching of Writing Division at the 1980 convention of the Modern Language Association. Under the leadership of Richard Lloyd-Jones, we executive committee members discussed our awareness of the increasing separation between composition and literature, our concern with that separation, and our feeling that such a gulf was detrimental to research in language as a whole and to the teaching of both composition and literature. We felt that our program at the 1981 convention could well address that concern and serve as a first step toward building a bridge between the two. This book came out of that decision and that first attempt to close the gap between literature and composition.

Since the inception of the Teaching of Writing Division, I have attended most of the sessions. In talking with the members of the division, the second largest of the association, I discovered that most were persons whose first interests were in literature and critical theory, but they had chosen the Teaching of Writing Division because they were, in fact, now seriously engaged in teaching composition. Most readily admitted that all their training had been in literature and that they attended the sessions to learn about research in the teaching of writing. The size of the division reflects dramatically the changing nature of our discipline and the evident fact that most of us, though trained in literature, are indeed teaching composition. This book is a response to that fact.

In reality, literature and composition cannot be separated either in theory or in teaching practice. Composition theory and critical theory are indeed opposite sides of the same coin, and the "teaching" of writing and the "teaching" of literature are applications of theories that are closely connected, often inseparable, and always fundamental to the study of language. Not only are composition theory and critical theory philosophically connected, but research in one can enlighten and enrich knowledge of the other.

The breach between literature and composition can be explained by a number of historical facts in the rhetoric tradition out of which the study of English arose. In the first place, language study under the rubric of rhetoric has always evinced lamentable tendencies to allow itself to be fragmented and to let its name be associated with the trivial and superficial aspects of the communication act. Divorced from its philosophic base, English rhetoric in the sixteenth century became almost exclusively associated with stylistic ornament. Out of this interest came hundreds of books that were little more than lists of figures, and rhetoric became almost entirely concerned with form. The elocutionary movement, which came to full bloom in the eighteenth and nineteenth centuries, was another example of fragmented rhetoric. Gestures and body movements were measurable physical phenomena, so graphing and measuring these elements fit in well with the scientific age. Unfortunately, freshman composition, as it is often taught, falls philosophically within the same class as elocution and stylistic rhetoric. With its emphasis on spelling, punctuation, and surface correctness, it too has often been a fragmented rhetoric of form without serious content. Such superficial matters have seldom engaged the attention of great scholars.

A second important historical fact is that the study of English literature, which grew out of the same tradition as elocution and stylistic rhetoric, is of recent origin. It was, in fact, in the middle of the nineteenth century in the Scottish universities that English studies first replaced the classics as the philosophic center of the curriculum. At Cambridge and Oxford English literature was not part of the official curriculum until after 1900. The study of Greek and Latin literature thrived in the British universities; English literature was the folk art of the vernacular and was considered, for the most part, unworthy of serious study. It was because of the popularity of the English literature lectures of William Edmonstoune Aytoun at the University of Edinburgh that the first professorship of English literature was established there in 1861. Francis Child was appointed the first professor of English literature at Harvard in 1869, though his work was mostly in philology. But these two universities were the innovators. In 1864 Oberlin College stated publicly that it considered Shakespeare unsuitable for classroom instruction. Oxford University did not have a chair of English literature until 1904, and when the Modern Language Association was established in 1883 the twenty largest universities in the United States had only thirty-nine English professors. Thus English literature is a comparatively new member of the academic community.

A third historical fact is that in the latter part of the eighteenth century and the beginning of the nineteenth there was a shift in the emphasis of rhetoric and language study from the creative act to the interpretive act. Until the eighteenth century, rhetoric had been largely the study of the generative act of composing. In its oldest tradition, rhetoric was concerned with discovering and communicating truth. Those arts and the teaching of those arts occupied some of the greatest minds in Western history—Plato, Aristotle, Augustine, and Francis Bacon. But at the Scottish universities in the eighteenth century, under the influence of such men as Adam Smith, Hugh Blair, and Henry Home, Lord Kames, the emphasis shifted from a study of the creative act to a study of reading, or the interpretive act. The movement started with the old terminology of rhetoric. It was the classical coin turned over. That emphasis has resulted in an impressive body of scholarship in critical theory in the nineteenth and twentieth centuries, but the name and terms have changed as literary scholars insist on dissociating themselves from the unsavory rhetoric of style, and of elocution, and of freshman composition.

One final fact about the rhetorical tradition and the study of English literature is that the early courses in English covered a far broader range of writings than those ordinarily included in the modern curriculum. David Masson, the great Milton scholar and the first regularly appointed professor of English literature at the University of Edinburgh, where he taught from 1865 to 1895, divided literature into four categories. The first category was history and biography, which he defined as "the biography of the body politic." The second and third were expository and didactic literature, which included oratorical or persuasive literature. And the fourth was "poetry and the literature of the imagination." Included in this early course on English literature were the writings of Isaac Newton and Joshua Reynolds.[1] Over the past hundred years the main research and teaching mission of the English discipline has been largely restricted to the final category—poetry and the literature of the imagination—while the study of expository and scientific writings is customarily assigned to the composition program and the term "imaginative" is denied to such works. It remains that almost three-fourths of what Professor Masson and his contemporaries taught as English literature has been eliminated from the main teaching and research thrust of the modern English department.

In these facts we can sketch the history of the breach, but we can only speculate as to the causes. A similar shift in interest from the creative act to the interpretive act took place in other disciplines—in music and the visual arts—and might be attributed partly to the rise of the universities in the latter part of the nineteenth century. Or the development of a literate culture through the dissemination of print might have encouraged such a change. We simply do not know. Why rhetoric tends to associate its name with form rather than with intellectual exploration, discovery, and serious content, which the best scholars of all ages have insisted are its province, remains in doubt. And, finally, it is not clear why the idea of literature as including only poetry and fiction has arisen in the past two centuries. The *Oxford English Dictionary* lists the definition of literature in the sense of "the body of writings produced in a particular country or period or in the world in general"—especially as "applied to writing which has claim to consideration on the ground of beauty of form or emotional effect"—as being of "very recent emergence both in English and French" and gives the first citation as 1812. We do not know the reasons for these historical facts. The effects, however, have been clear—the gulf between literature and composition has widened.

There are more recent causes for the breach; some came out of purely practical situations, but all together have formed a vicious circle. As enrollments increased, particularly at the American universities toward the end of the nineteenth century, English

1. University of Edinburgh, MS Gen. 1401:03.

professors found themselves spending an inordinate amount of time marking student themes. Albert Kitzhaber points out that at Michigan in 1894–95, 1,198 students were instructed by a staff of four full-time teachers and two part-time graduate assistants. Even at Harvard, where the student/professor ratio was lower, "there was much dissatisfaction there over English A, the required course in freshman composition, which it was thought took a dispro-portionate amount of staff time and labor."[2] In Scotland, Professor Aytoun complained that he had "enough student papers to roast an ox." Grading student themes has never been a chosen occu-pation, but complaining about freshmen's inability to write has always been a favorite coffee-room pastime. A good solution for both problems, it was felt, as it still is today, would be to delegate instruction in writing to the lower schools, or to graduate students, or to adjunct part-time faculty.

The results in larger universities were not unexpected. The senior tenured faculty continued to teach and pursue research in literature while the graduate students taught composition—but studied literature. After graduation, they gratefully abandoned the teaching of composition (with its onerous hours of theme grading and its ill-prepared students) and turned to serious re-search and teaching in literature. This group of graduates who came out of English doctoral programs in the sixties are part of our regular faculties today, many of them once again teaching freshman composition.

At smaller private four-year colleges, full-time faculty occa-sionally still taught the composition courses, but as enrollments increased they were more often turned over to graduate students from nearby universities or to other part-time faculty. At some large community colleges, composition teachers were hired from the community—many taught a course during lunch hour to earn extra Christmas money.

Historically, administrators at institutions of higher education in the United States did nothing to change a situation that for them held obvious economic advantages. Graduate students and temporary part-time teachers are notoriously cheap help, and the required composition program is a large and expensive proposi-tion. Furthermore, the senior members of English departments appeared to approve the teaching arrangement. In the larger uni-

2. Albert Raymond Kitzhaber, "Rhetoric in American Colleges 1850–1900," Ph.D. diss., University of Washington, 1953, 73.

versities the graduate students who were paid to teach freshman writing courses were also filling the senior professors' graduate seminars, and in smaller colleges the use of adjunct faculty freed the senior faculty to teach literature. But where did these senior faculty members come from, with their literature orientation and their disdain for teaching composition?

They came, in fact, from our own Ph.D. programs. Anyone who has been associated with graduate students in English over the past twenty years can attest to the metamorphosis that takes place as they earn doctorates. They enter the graduate program as teaching assistants excited about the possibilities of teaching composition. They want very much to do well, searching the literature and questioning their colleagues about teaching methods—in the time left over from their literature studies. During their four or five years in the program, the message is gradually but firmly conveyed that the serious business of the department is not research or teaching in composition but research and teaching in literary studies. They are given neither the encouragement nor the time to pursue research in rhetoric or composition theory—in fact, they are actively discouraged from spending time on composition, and they learn early how to cut corners. Finally, teaching composition becomes a dreary task. They long to teach the literature courses for which their years of study have prepared them. These graduate students are part of our regular faculty today—many of them now once again teaching freshman composition. And the vicious circle is complete.

And so the historical gulf widens. Composition research, understandably, has until very recently not been encouraged or even tolerated in departments of English. For years such research has been carried on in schools of education and has been largely concerned with pedagogy at the lower school level. Maverick English professors who pursued research in composition theory or the teaching of composition did so at their peril. For years many departments made it clear to their junior members that promotion and tenure would not be awarded on the basis of research in composition. Many departments still do so, though such prejudices are seldom publicly stated. Cases of assistant professors' being hired to direct or work in the composition program (since administrators seldom deny funds for composition positions) and then being told that their research must be in literary studies are common. As the message sinks in, their interests return to literature, and both they and their departments conveniently forget that the funding was for a rhetoric-composition position. These cases are classic and legion. Only very committed and competent researchers can resist such pressures in the present job market. Many departments prefer a second-class Milton scholar to a composition researcher. Such members do not threaten the department's literary thrust.

In the 1970s the situation in the English discipline changed drastically, again for a number of pragmatic reasons. As the post–World War II baby-boom babies grew up and graduated from colleges across the nation, enrollments at large universities dropped or leveled off, and, worse still for the humanities, students turned to more practical degrees that would ensure them a share of the dollar pie. Literature study had little to offer these business-oriented students of the seventies. The preferred professions were medicine, law, and engineering.

These circumstances, predictably, had profound effects on English departments. As enrollments dropped at all levels, positions were cut and hundreds of English Ph.D.s vied for the few openings available. Many failed to find jobs. At the same time that literature enrollments dropped, enrollments in writing courses increased. In many cases administrators withdrew funds from literature programs and added them to writing projects. Senior scholars who had not taught writing since their graduate-school days were forced to teach composition when their seminars failed to "make." Men and women who had devoted their professional lives to the study of literature now found that their field of expertise was considered expendable. These senior scholars understandably feel threatened, angry, and deeply discouraged.

Another group in the English discipline that has been seriously affected by the drop in enrollment in literature courses and the concomitant increases in composition are the junior members of English departments. In most cases their entire Ph.D. training has been in literary studies, but, if they are fortunate enough to obtain university positions, all or a large portion of their teaching will be in composition. With their literature backgrounds, they are ill inclined and ill suited to that task. These young scholars, too, often are deeply discouraged about their professional futures.

This book is for those members of our profession, both young and old, whose primary interests may be in either composition or literary theory but who are teaching composition. Represented within these pages are a few of those committed composition scholars who, in spite of the English discipline's history of professional isolation and stigma for their work, have produced solid research in both literature and composition. Also represented here are members of another growing group, those outstanding literary scholars who recognize the importance of teaching composition and are themselves adding to the body of research in that field. Their presence here eloquently attests that research in composition is alive and growing, and that both literary and composition scholars of the highest caliber are beginning to contribute to it.

Included here are men and women who approach the gulf between composition and literature with different points of view. All of them are well-known scholars in English language and literature. All deny that they are specialists in either composition or literature. They all see their work as bridging the gap—their research in literature and composition is part of their total professional commitment. Finally, all of them teach both writing and literature with success and satisfaction.

This book is an attempt to uncover fresh and exciting opportunities within our profession. It sees, through the eyes of the scholars represented here, that the division between composition and literature is truly a matter of attitude and history and that in joining forces we can find the strength and the resources to forge new directions for the discipline. It is, finally, an attempt to reintroduce respectability to the teaching of writing and to return us, as scholars and teachers to a concern with composition theory and the creative act.

In a period when the discipline of English and also the humanities in general are being examined and their value questioned, these twelve men and women address the issues. In the essays that follow, leaders in the profession present the problems as they see them and, while recognizing that there are no simple solutions, discuss the future and suggest challenging new directions.

The Contributors

Richard A. Lanham is professor of English and executive director of the writing programs at the University of California at Los Angeles. He has written a number of books and articles on rhetoric and has maintained a continuing interest in critical theory and style in both historical and contemporary writing. His most recent works are *Revising Prose* (New York: Scribner's, 1979), *Revising Business Prose* (New York: Scribner's, 1981), and *Analyzing Prose* (New York: Scribner's, forthcoming). Professor Lanham describes the literacy crisis caused by the radically changing student population of our colleges and universities and suggests that it presents literary studies with an "enormous problem" that may redeem "both our teaching and our research and put literary study back in the center of modern humanism where in our hearts we know it belongs."

Josephine Miles is professor of English at the University of California at Berkeley and author of a dozen volumes of verse, the most recent being *Coming to Terms* (Urbana: University of Illinois Press, 1979), and of histories of language in poetry, like *Poetry and Change* (Berkeley: University of California Press, 1974). Professor Miles is also a veteran in the teaching of composition, as exemplified by her essays in *Working out Ideas* (Berkeley: Bay Area Writer's Project, 1979). Here, she plays with an idea she obviously takes most seriously, that the working parts of a sentence are beautifully simple and usable in an age predictably concerned with computing, word processing, and sentence generating. Professor Miles uses a series of well-chosen jokes and riddles as persuasive examples of compositional patterning.

J. Hillis Miller is the Frederick W. Hilles Professor of English and Comparative Literature at Yale and director of the Literature Major, an experimental undergraduate major in reading and writing. He is the author of numerous books and articles on nineteenth- and twentieth-century English and American literature and on literary criticism, most recently of *Fiction and Repetition: Seven English Novels* (Cambridge: Harvard University Press, 1982). Professor Miller makes a strong argument for not detaching programs in composition from departments of English, but he advises "the theorists of literature . . . to face the practical implications for the teaching of writing as well as for the teaching of reading of their theories, and the teachers of writing . . . to be as clear as possible about the theoretical assumptions of what they do." In his examination of some of the theories behind deconstruction, and especially in a discussion of metaphor and tropes, he maintains that "reading is itself a kind of writing, or writing is a trope for the act of reading. Every act of writing is an act of reading, an interpretation of some part of the totality of what is."

Wayne C. Booth has published a number of books on rhetoric and critical theory, including *The Rhetoric of Fiction* (Chicago: University of Chicago Press, 1961), *A Rhetoric of Irony* (Chicago: University of Chicago Press, 1974), *Modern Dogma and the Rhetoric of Assent* (Chicago: University of Chicago Press, 1974), and *Critical Understanding: The Powers and Limits of Pluralism* (Chicago: University of Chicago Press, 1979). "All of my books," he says, "even the last and most abstract, profit directly from my regular teaching of literature *and* composition to beginning students." At Earlham College (as chairman, for nine years) and at the University of Chicago (as professor for twenty years, five of them as dean of the College) he has taught "more undergraduates than graduates, more LITCOMP courses than any other kind." In outlining his course, Booth suggests that literature be included, but he questions the "relatively narrow conception of literature" that informs most English departments today. Professor Booth's proposed course, as outlined here, is clearly a course *in* rhetoric as a bridge between "lit" and "comp," but it is at the same time an invitation to the process of redefining that "radically ambiguous term."

David Bleich is professor of English at Indiana University at Bloomington. His research has been in reading theory, and he has published numerous articles in that field. His most recent book is *Subjective Criticism* (Baltimore: Johns Hopkins University Press, 1978). Professor Bleich discusses a new conception of, and a new attitude toward, language. Language use is studied as it appears in two contexts that are understood as predicated on one another: naming and discussing historical life experience, and identifying one's subjective experience of symbolic objects (literature in this case).

Nancy Comley is director of freshman English in the Department of English at Queens College of the City University of New York. She has written a number of journal articles and is editor of the poetry section of Oxford University Press's *Elements of Literature* (1982), edited by Carl H. Klaus, Michael Silverman, and her coauthor in the essay that follows. Robert Scholes is professor of English and comparative literature and director of the semiotics program at Brown University. He is the author of a number of books on literary theory and coauthor with Professor Comley of *The Practice of Writing: An Introduction to the Forms of Discourse* (New York: St. Martin's Press, 1981). Professors Comley and Scholes insist that the opposition between literature and composition must be broken down. They present a sketch of how that can be done theoretically, followed by some examples from their own teaching experience of how it can be accomplished in classroom practice.

Elaine P. Maimon directs the writing across the curriculum program which she initiated at Beaver College, where she is also an associate dean and associate professor of English. During the 1982–83 academic year she is a visiting associate professor of English at the University of Pennsylvania. With four colleagues representing a variety of disciplines, she has written two composition textbooks, *Writing in the Arts and Sciences* (Boston: Little, Brown, 1981), and *Readings in the Arts and Sciences* (Boston: Little, Brown, 1984). As a member of the National Endowment for the Humanities National Board of Consultants, she has advised many colleges and universities on ways to bridge the gap between literature and composition. Professor Maimon explores the concept of genre and its pertinence to reading, writing, and thinking within various disciplines, and within the academic community as a whole.

Walter J. Ong, S.J., is William E. Haren Professor of English and professor of humanities in psychiatry at Saint Louis University and a past president of the Modern Language Association (1978). He is the author of numerous books and articles on Renaissance literary and intellectual history, and on rhetoric and the evolution of consciousness from antiquity to the present. Three of his more recent works, *Interfaces of the Word* (Ithaca: Cornell University Press, 1977), *The Presence of the Word* (New Haven: Yale University Press, 1967; paperback, Minneapolis: University of Minnesota Press, 1981), and *Rhetoric, Romance, and Technology* (Ithaca: Cornell University Press, 1971), trace the alienation and reintegration of consciousness brought about through technological transformations of the word by writing, print, and electronics and the effects of the transformations on oral tradition and literary forms, on thought processes, and on social structures and behavior. Here Professor Ong discusses the differences between literacy and orality and the confusing complex patterns set up in contemporary culture by the vigorous interaction between a residual primary orality, literacy, and secondary orality.

E. D. Hirsch, Jr., is chairman of the Department of English at the University of Virginia. His work includes numerous writings on theory of criticism, on European and English romanticism, and on theory of composition. His best-known works are *Validity in Interpretation* (New Haven: Yale University Press, 1967), *The Aims of Interpretation* (Chicago: University of Chicago Press, 1976), and *The Philosophy of Composition* (Chicago: University of Chicago Press, 1977). Here he rethinks some of his conclusions in *The Philosophy of Composition* and argues that competence in reading or in writing depends on a "cultural literacy." "Illiteracy then, is not merely a deficiency in reading and writing skills . . . but also a deficiency in cultural information." He sees the teaching of cultural information, however, as a goal of all teaching in high schools and colleges, not of English departments alone.

Davis S. Kaufer is director of the freshman writing program at Carnegie-Mellon University. His research includes work on the theory of argument, linguistics, the composing process, and applications of the computer to rhetorical studies. Richard E. Young is head of the English Department at Carnegie-Mellon University. His research has centered on the theory and pedagogy of rhetorical invention and the composing process. Professors Kaufer and Young identify two theories of art underlying current teaching of writing in English departments and discuss the implications these theories have for teaching and for educational policy. They conclude by asking whether English departments are ready to support two disciplines rather than one discipline and a service function.

Frederick Crews is professor of English at the University of California at Berkeley, where he has been chairman of his department's freshman composition program. He is the author of numerous critical and popular books, including *The Pooh Perplex: A Freshman Casebook* (New York: Dutton, 1963) and the widely used text *The Random House Handbook*, whose fourth edition will appear in 1984. Professor Crews acknowledges the long-standing antagonism between professors of composition and professors of literature. Presenting what he calls a "minimal" case, he recommends the use of literary readings in freshman English "to improve the morale and thereby the effectiveness of freshman English." He concludes by introducing as "a point at least worth debating" that composition, instead of being taught as a separate discipline, "should be diffused through courses possessing their own intrinsic interest and their own well-delineated academic idiom."

Edward P. J. Corbett, professor of English at Ohio State University, has published widely in both composition and literature, seeing rhetoric as the bridge between the two. His *Classical Rhetoric for the Modern Student*, 2d ed. (New York: Oxford University Press, 1971) has become a familiar work for teachers and students of rhetoric and composition at all levels. He was also editor of *College Composition and Communication* and chairman of the Rhetoric Society of America, and he served on the National Council of Teachers of English Commission on Composition. He directed the freshman English program at Creighton University in Omaha, Nebraska, from 1953 to 1966 and that at Ohio State University from 1966 to 1970. He speaks not only as a well-known scholar in both literature and composition but also as an experienced writing-program administrator. Professor Corbett defines the issues and traces the historical developments of the division. He then marshals a series of arguments, some from his own experience, for relegating literature and composition to separate classrooms, a view opposed to that expressed by Frederick Crews in this volume. Professor Corbett concludes, however, that language, literature, and composition must remain three "related, coordinate, and complementary parts" of the English discipline.

1   One, Two, Three
Richard A. Lanham

One: What is the relationship between teaching literature and teaching composition?

Two: Should English departments take an interest in teaching composition?

Three: How does question one relate to question two?

"Bombs educate vigorously," Henry Adams maintained. Population bombs, apparently, do not have the same effect. Although several have hit English studies in the past twenty years, we seem to have learned very little. First, the baby boom that followed the Second World War prompted us to assume that enrollments that go up will never come down. After that bubble burst, a series of social and demographic changes brought more black and Hispanic and, in California, Asian-American students into our teaching lives, but this fundamental change has prompted no fresh thinking that I can detect. And now have come the current waves of immigration that are bringing more first-generation Spanish-speaking students, more first-generation Asian immigrants speaking a dozen different languages, more Middle Eastern students, and so on. While these chasms grow ever wider, and partly because of them, the American system of public education has broken down completely and the fifty-hour television week has stepped in to fill the void. To gift wrap such alarms and excursions, the world during these twenty years has become, through revolutions in trade, energy, and communications, a genuinely global society. European culture has ceased to be the defining focus for Western thought, and, yet more important for English studies, England has ceased to be the defining focus for America's connection with Europe. Finally, during these years what promises to be the biggest bomb of all has sneaked up on us—the computer revolution. The written and the read word have suffered, in their whole manner of existence, a radical electronic transmogrification.

English studies, meanwhile, has matured the disciplinary focus begun with the foundation of the Oxford English School in 1894. The critics and the philologists, after a long period of guerrilla warfare, stand more or less at peace, *aequo Marte;* the discipline has divided itself into specializations by period, genre, and great figure; it has developed bibliographical procedures that allow it to treat English texts with biblical scrupulosity; and, most important, it has developed a critical philosophy that sanctifies its departmental and disciplinary status. The argument that literature constitutes a reality apart from ordinary reality, deserving of study in and for itself, was present from the first, though for a long time it was exemplified by only a very few men (most notably Ernest de Selincourt in England and Thomas Lounsbury in America). The argument came into its own with the New Criticism, of course, and later with the work of Northrop Frye and others. And, although the "privilege" of literary discourse has now come into question, it is fair to say that "literary" truth as distinct from scientific truth still prevails as the reigning assumption. It is this assumption that legitimates literature as a subject to be studied for its own sake.

This process of disciplinary growth has now reached full self-conscious maturity: practitioners in the field are reflecting self-consciously on the boundary conditions of their own activity, anatomizing it into its careerist, gamelike, and creative aspects. The maturation was accelerated by the two go-go decades of academic prosperity from 1955 to 1975, a flood of students and money that released English studies not only from composition instruction, until then its historic base in America, but also from routine instruction in the lower division. The discipline was thus freed to draw in upon itself, become graduate- and professional-centered, and sponsor metalevel reflections upon literary texts and inquiry—upon, that is, itself.

These years brought an impressive improvement in the quality and sophistication of literary training. Many bright people came into the profession and suffused it with their wit and ambition. Although occasionally diverted for a moment by the social explosions of those years, for the most part the discipline matured in a self-enclosed way. Self-enclosure was, after all, its enfranchising assumption. And this concentrated attention produced not only a *Blumzeit* of literary criticism but a concomitant maturity in bibliographical and linguistic and philological inquiry as well. No knowledgeable person would want to belittle, or to damage, this powerful maturity in the discipline. But, as we are now finding out, such maturity assumed a specific social base—the reigning society, in fact, when the Oxford English School was founded in 1894: white, literate, and at least middle class.

English studies now provides a superb instrument to educate such a society. That society, alas, no longer exists. The society in which English studies must function, in America at least, is no longer predominantly middle and upper middle class, nor is the dwindling white segment of it any longer reliably literate. English studies, like so many armies in the past, now stands superbly equipped to fight the last war.

Meanwhile, as this disciplinary Maginot Line was being brought to perfection, there was poor old English comp. Composition was all that English studies had striven for a hundred years not to be. Avowedly a "service department," it had no room of its own either in theory or in practice. The very opposite of self-enclosed, it served as time and circumstance dictated. Freshman writing, technical writing, business writing, legal writing—you name it and comp people would try to do it. Because the teaching loads and strains were desperately high, nobody went into comp who didn't have to or stayed any longer than forced to. These unwilling instructors might not have much theory, but they did know what their students were like. They were not fooled by the sixties' genial fantasy of "the best-educated generation in American history." They knew a big problem was coming and was going to last a long time.

Now it has come, and comp is prospering—even getting a room of its own—and English studies wonders what it should think and do about it.

We have, on the one hand, a powerfully mature discipline and its concomitant career game, with a sharply dwindling demand for its services as it chooses to define them. On the other hand, we have an enormous social need for instruction in language, a need that will continue, whether enrollments in English pick up or not, for at least a generation. Can we get these two worlds together? Use the talents and methods of English studies to address the literacy crisis? Conversely, can we use the literacy crisis to support English studies through lean times and preserve this discipline it has taken a century to define?

Opinions differ. At one end of the spectrum stand the *aboutistes* in literary studies. They will have nothing to do with comp— that way lies the old "service department" routine. Fix up the schools and let them do it. It is not the university's business. At the opposite extreme stand the comp conservatives who want nothing to do with literature. They can be old veterans who resent the incursion of the "literati" into their lower-class but sometimes well-paying turf; they can be new-minted theorists who want to reinvent for composition the theory literary criticism has spent the past hundred years working out. Both groups want to go the route literary studies began in 1894. They want a room, a department of their own. They don't want to convince the literature people to teach comp. To hell with them. Comp is not their department, at least not anymore. In midspectrum lurk a few puzzled folk trying to explore what the relationships are, or should be, between these two areas of teaching and inquiry.

There are two ways to ask this question: (1) What is the relationship between teaching literature and teaching composition? (2) Should English departments take an interest in teaching composition?

Literature people characteristically formulate the question in the first way, composition types in the second. The first way looks inward to theory, the second outward to the pressures of an "insistent present." The first question turns out, in broad outline, to be easily answered, and the second proves no more difficult, though needing a longer answer. The really vexing question turns out to be a third—the relation between the first and the second.

One

The first question asks, "What is the relationship between teaching literature and teaching composition?"

The history of twentieth-century English studies suggests an answer. That history chronicles the search for a literary theory that would legitimate English studies as an independent discipline. The resulting theory argued that literature should constitute an independent inquiry because its pseudostatements presented an independent order of truth. This legitimating departmental premise has surfaced in several guises since its synthesis from Renaissance golden poetics and its rebirth in Coleridgian thinking.

If this theory is true, or assumed to be, no English department can bear an intrinsic relation to composition teaching. However comp goes about its business, comp is about communication in the "real" world—"out there." It deals with nonprivileged texts, with "prose" rather than "poetry." To define literature as privileged by implication defines composition in an opposite way. Composition becomes the study of communication in a world posited to be "real," admittedly "out there," in contradistinction to literature's imaginative reality. What I have called the clarity-brevity-sincerity or "CBS" theory of prose style follows understandably from such an assumption.

In such a polarized orchestration, English departments will preoccupy themselves with the visionary moral order literature is thought to present. The composition section will teach an "effective communication" tailored to context. This division of labor represents pretty much where we are now. *Or at least where we think we are*. For if this conception of literature is incomplete and misguided, then the state of affairs it implies can never in fact happen. At best it can only half happen. Literature can never absent itself from the "real" world, nor can composition do without literature and literary criticism.

So let's sketch out the opposite case. Here literature does not constitute a separate reality. Life here is full of "literary" elements. We might picture the relation of "literature" to "life" as a spectrum. At one end of the spectrum stands neutral "real life," detached from man and his recreative imagination. At the other end that recreative imagination stands by itself, detached from flesh-and-blood reality, a world of fantasy.

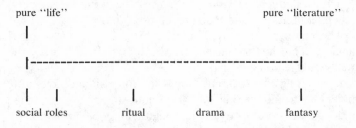

But there are all kinds of mixed states in the middle. Most of what we call reality, in this way of understanding the problem, is "literary" to one degree or another. And of course one could construct a similar spectrum for the perceiver rather than for the perceived.

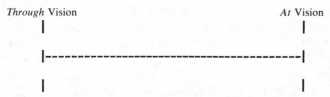

Through Vision   *At* Vision

At the left extreme, we are never self-conscious about the act of seeing or reading; we read only "for information." At the right extreme, we read or see only for style, look *at* a visual or verbal surface rather than *through* it. On neither spectrum is "literature" all one kind of experience and "life" all another. And the extremes on each spectrum are asymptotic; no pure cases exist. In this orchestration, literature does not stand apart from "reality"; it constitutes and suffuses it, much as role playing constitutes social reality.

If this conception of literature is accepted, it brings along with it a different conception of self and of social reality, as so much of contemporary sociology and cultural anthropology makes clear. And it changes how we think about composition. The CBS theory now covers only a restricted range of prose composition. A resolute insistence on transparent prose gives way to a symbiotic exchange in which a prose surface both creates the reality beneath and in turn is affected by it. I've argued this case in *Style: An Anti-textbook* and need not repeat it here. But the main point must be made: in this alternative conception of literature and of composition *the problematic relationship between the two simply disappears*. They represent different points on the same series of spectra. No difference *in kind* exists between them. Teaching literature and teaching composition form different parts of the same activity.

English departments, then, find themselves trapped in a paradox. To preserve their discipline, they may have to interest themselves in composition. But if they do they must discard their legitimating premise as a separate field of inquiry.

Two

What, now, if we ask our basic question in its practical form: "Should English departments take an interest in teaching composition?" For many departments, to be sure, this question no longer makes sense. They may not be *interested in* composition, but they have *become* departments of composition. For them teaching literature performs, statistically if not emotionally, a secondary function. The meaningful questions for them are "Can we learn to like what we have to do anyway?" "How can we harmonize these two endeavors?" But there are departments that do not face this *argumentum ad baculum*. Not many, but some. For them the question occurs in its pure form: "Is there any reason English departments should be interested in composition if they don't have to be?" What answer can we give? Well, first we can admit candidly that there are some compelling reasons they *should not* take an interest in the problem. The theoretical paradox just examined, for one: an interest in comp threatens the English department's legitimating premise. Practical problems threaten as well. Teaching literature, for most who do it, proves self-renewing. It is no mere cliché that one returns from teaching and reading Chaucer or Shakespeare excited and rejuvenated. Each return to the text offers further vision into it. Such study *is* self-renewing. For most people, teaching composition does not bring the same renewal. Composition teaching remains repetitive and routine. It also takes grotesque amounts of time. If you do it for long uninterrupted, it threatens to turn your mind to oatmeal. It is no good pretending this isn't so. One of the main problems of composition teaching is just this burnout. How can you design a program that avoids it? One that renews the teacher in a cybernetically stable way as literature does?

Beyond this unmarked crossroads lurks another tar baby. Get interested in composition and you'll find yourself in administration. It comes with the job. The teaching of writing, in the present general campus scene, involves an incredible amount of liaison and planning, far more than a ten-week bout with "English Drama to 1649." This time has to come from somewhere.

Still another problem. As electronic communications technology develops, comp programs will become heavily involved in it. It will stand at the center of what they do. But how do you factor into the regular career pattern of English studies the computer specialists, television producers, systems analysts, and statisticians needed for a large-scale campuswide composition program? For these and many other reasons, a strong case, both theoretical and practical, can be made for keeping literature teaching distinct from composition.

Can an equally strong case be made for bringing the two activities together? Again, first theory and then practice.

Theory. I've argued that the definition of literature that legitimates English studies as an independent discipline—its departmental license—must be discarded if comp is to share more than a Xerox machine with literary study. Strong reasons, even aside from the composition problem, suggest that this required theoretical change might be good for English studies. They suggest, too, a new kind of departmental franchise.

To conceive of literary texts as constituting a separate reality is also to conceive of a positivistic social reality just "out there" and a self just "in here," halfway between the ears. Both concepts have been discarded by almost every other discipline that deals with human behavior. Literary critics who still think this way thus find themselves at war with the rest of the curriculum: with the sociologist who examines role theory; with the cultural anthropologist who finds "ordinary" communication astoundingly full of literary ingredients; with the perception psychologist who stresses the active, participating, integrative role of perception (a role that makes nonsense of the CBS theory of prose style, for example), and above all with those who study the social behavior of animals and are finding the sources of literature's mythic energy not in a mystic visionary imagination but in the deeply layered, fundamentally nonintelligent depths of the limbic system. Although I haven't time to spell it out here, a new and genuinely post-Darwinian conception of humanism is right now emerging in all the disciplines that study *Homo sapiens.* If the comp problem were to force a paradigm change in English studies, one that enabled it to join this new consensus, that change alone would make the composition crisis worth facing—even, perhaps especially, in departments that can afford to ignore it.

Practice. The two fields obviously overlap in day-to-day teaching and research—in linguistics, philology, and so on—but we need not linger here when larger issues merit attention. The first of these issues—the undergraduate curriculum—derives directly from our theoretical discussion. The disintegration of the undergraduate curriculum has now been universally remarked. It lacks any legitimating premise except *chacun à son gout.* The current attempts to restore it by reinstating the old breadth requirements, and their attendant stale clichés, will all fail. They depend on the same dead paradigm for social behavior that keeps English literature and English composition facing in opposite directions. The new humanist consensus, based as it must be on evolutionary biology—based, that is, on new, genuinely legitimating behavioral premises—will really refound the undergraduate curriculum. Literature departments must choose whether to join this new curriculum and try to assert their centrality within it or whether, like classics, to paint themselves into their own quiet corner.

The felt center for studying man is shifting from the traditional humanities to other disciplines in much the same way that the traditional European focus for Western thought has now diffused throughout the globe. In my own field of classical rhetoric, for example, the exciting discoveries now come from primatology and evolutionary biology and genetics, not from the academic discipline of rhetoric. That discipline does not even know it has been usurped. It continues, with a kind of genial, knee-jerk antiquarianism, to—if I may borrow C. S. Lewis's wonderful phrase—"leave no corpse ungalvanized." Meanwhile, life and hope have marshaled elsewhere. If literary studies really should stand at the center of a humanist curriculum—and I think they should—they must be prepared to explain how and why this should be so, not simply mouth stale clichés based on a dead paradigm.

But a chance to join the new humanist curriculum not only means a new legitimating premise for the department, it means a new day-to-day working sense of what a department is and how it relates to other departments. For a model we might glance at a discipline like biology that, unlike our own, has fully participated in the neo-Darwinian synthesis. The "department" there is clearly fissionable material, an ad hoc structure that tries to change, subdivide, and readjust to a developing, expanding body of knowledge. At least in the biology departments I know about, the result has been radical and nervous structural reorganization. We need the same thing in English studies. Coming to terms with composition is our best chance to bring it about. The department system, which began at Harvard in 1825 and really caught on at the end of the nineteenth century, has now a long evolutionary history. It works best as it has worked in English studies, when it presides over the *genesis* of a discipline, provides the focus early growth requires. But in maturity it can strangle the discipline it was created to preserve. Decisions are taken for the health of the *department*—a derivative, ancillary unit, remember—and not for the growth of the discipline. When you get this far you are

polishing a dead paradigm. It is arguable, I think, that English
studies has now gotten this far. Certainly many departments have.

English studies can, then, choose a voice in the new humanism
or run back to the old. We face the same choice, on a larger scale,
in choosing our role in a multiracial and multilingual America.
An English department's sense of itself, its whole manner of proceeding, depends on a society monolingual in English and idiom-
atically so. That monolingualism is now changing. Some regions
feel the change more than others, but in some degree it will come
to everyone. The most obvious rebellion comes in the broad band
of Hispanic culture that now runs from southern California across
the Southwest, skips up to Chicago and then down to Florida,
then runs northward to New York and beyond. In California the
Asian-American population provides an obvious second instance;
in other places, other groups—the West Indian population in To-
ronto, for example. For the whole country, of course, the native
black dialect remains a persistent, if partial, exception to the
monolingual premise. Most of these groups are reproducing themselves in greater numbers than the Anglo population and presumably will continue to do so. And over these broad homegrown
population changes we must now layer the waves of immigrants
reaching our shores. To take as an example my own home ground,
Los Angeles now has the largest Korean community outside Ko-
rea, the largest Armenian community in America, a large Iranian
community, more than one hundred thousand Egyptians, the largest Polynesian community outside Polynesia, well over one
hundred thousand Vietnamese, and now a daily influx of Central
American political refugees. When earlier waves of immigration
hit America, it was a far different America. The melting pot was
still supposed to melt; there was no talk on Ellis Island about the
right to one's own language. A low-technology agricultural society
offered menial and unskilled jobs. There was a lot of vacant land
and of first-generation industrial growth to act as a cushion. All
this absorbent circumstance has now changed, and the language
problems have gotten worse—more languages, more different *kinds*
of language, and all coming at once.

To such a population, the study of English, and even American,
literature is bound to seem alien. For most of them, and for at
least a generation, current spoken English will seem difficult
enough, and earlier stages of the language—the Shakespearian
and Chaucerian versions I customarily teach, for example—

impossibly remote. Most of these students, when they reach the university, are not going to major in English. They'll study English composition, if we make them, but not English literature. Let me give you another California example. Twenty percent of the undergraduates at Berkeley and 24 percent of those at UCLA are now of Asian-American descent. Of this group, only 6 percent major in a humanistic discipline of any kind. By the end of the decade, projections suggest that 50 percent of the Berkeley undergraduates will be Asian students, but the humanistic 6 percent of them presumably will remain the same. What does this promise for English enrollments?

But enrollments only introduce us to the real problem. It will be a good while before many of the new ethnic groups come to the university in force. (That underrepresentation, of course, presents its own grave problems, political and ideological.) The larger question is what role English studies wants to take in a multilingual society. Shall we sit back and assume that the American pressures for monolingualism will solve our problems? Bring us back to the status quo ante? Should we try to train the teachers upon whom this monolingualizing burden will largely fall? That would mean a marked departure from our present practice. Or shall we be content, as may happen, to shrink into a much smaller discipline, an Anglo Studies Center in a country no longer predominantly Anglo?

The choice depends on the relation with composition. If we choose an active strategy, try to train the imagination of a multilingual society, composition must play a fundamental part in the endeavor. A passive, monastic strategy leads the other way, toward the old self-enclosed paradigm and departmental self-conception. Choosing an active role brings with it many present dangers: uncertainties of training and evaluation, mistakes attendant on new categories of teaching, new applications of what we already know, strange new areas of research. These dangers should not be ignored. They will inevitably blur the focus and disturb the balance of the present departmental and disciplinary structure. But the passive monastic strategy brings dangers too. Dwindling disciplines usually become sterile, ineffectual, and querulous. As their sense of breadth and purpose shrinks, morale drops and defensiveness increases. A rancid, Luddite, coterie mentality develops. The humanist disciplines abound in this Luddite resentment already. If we decide to hide, it can only get worse.

The relation with composition stands, then, at the center of the basic decisions for English studies: the decision about its place in the humanist curriculum and the decision about its place in a multilingual America. In both cases these decisions are going to be made. In the past they have been made for us by a dominant tradition. Not so today. America will have to *decide* on its linguistic reality and *decide* on its definition of man. If English studies wants to take a hand in these decisions, it will have to take an interest in composition. These are not Hobson's choices forced upon us by enrollment pressure. These are broad, considered policy decisions, the decisions humanists are supposed to be especially good at making.

A third decision impends, too, one that comprehends the other two. It is now daily front-page news that the orderly sequence of American education has broken down. The three Rs usually make the headlines, but the decay of study in other disciplines—history, for example—has been at least as grave. College students read and write like high-school sophomores, law students (if you are lucky) like freshmen; a high-school principal crows with glee when his graduating seniors read at ninth-grade level. The educational sequence in America has, of course, been notoriously disorderly and discontinuous. In a developing America realizing itself westward, such discontinuity literally came with the territory. What is happening now is more than more of the same. The social breakdown of the schools is profound and well documented, but the intellectual breakdown is even worse. The teaching of literature, our immediate concern, is desperately haphazard and ill informed. Here a lonely traditional devotee labors to teach Thomas Hardy to an uncomprehending class of world refugees, there a sixties' veteran trooper tries to get a class into *Soul on Ice*.

And the teaching of writing is, if anything, worse than the teaching of literature. How could it be otherwise? Most of these teachers have not been trained to teach either literature or composition. Teacher training is, after all, the first thing an ambitious English department gets rid of. The teachers labor with incredible courage and devotion in their impossible new world, without even a training adequate for the old-fashioned possible one.

This pathological lack of orderly sequence demands remedy. We can't, though, restore the old status quo. Too much has changed. And who in God's name would want to restore it anyway? The new one, for English, must combine language and literature studies in new ways, ways often using electronic intermediation, for a start. If the schools' curriculum is not restored, the college curriculum will continue a patchwork of short-term remediation and long-term confusion. Equally clear, if the schools don't take a directive role in the multilinguistic babble, somebody else—business, probably—will step in, the schools will get vouchered out of existence, and the university curriculum will become a total shambles. Both of our larger issues, then—the humanist curriculum and a national language policy—depend finally on restoring an orderly educational sequence in the schools. At the center of this restoration must stand English and mathematics. Should the well-bred English department take a hand in this restoration? If so, the way in, as in the other two areas, lies through composition. There's where the action is and has been. That's where people are already engaged with the problem. English departments can shape and influence a new English sequence, or they can sit back and carp when the job is done—by someone else—so much worse than they could have done it.

Composition, then, embodies the basic choices English departments must make in the next decade. Not only enrollment pressures stand at issue, but fundamental strategic choices. Circumstances will dictate different choices for different departments. At the center of them all, however, stands a fundamental problem. And this problem, paradoxically, and with a nice compensatory, egalitarian logic, affects departments more, the *more* research oriented they are, the *more* remote they are, or think themselves, from the literacy crisis. The fear composition instruction inspires in polite English departments derives partly, as I noted earlier, from the nonrenewing nature of the teaching. But even more it stems from a threat to accepted patterns of research. Much research in composition has been trivial and jejune, but even had it been better, it has often been of the wrong kind— research about pedagogy, about administration, about the delivery systems that socialize knowledge rather than about the research endeavors that synthesize it. It is this threat of *applied* research that, as comp has grown, has sparked so much fear and suspicion. It is just here, at the pure applied interface, that the problem needs thinking out.

A university research career, whatever the field, is animated by three kinds of motive: *Practical purpose*—How do you kill the tobacco budworm but not the tobacco? *Competition*—How

can I beat Linus Pauling to the Nobel Prize? And *pure play*—
How can I design a simple cubical puzzle that will drive the
puzzle-solving world crazy and yet not be actually unsolvable?
Different times, different places, and different disciplines have
mixed these basic motives in different ways. Practical purpose
presides over agriculture schools, though rivalry is not unknown
there. Competition usually supplies the principal propellant in law
schools. The humanities have chosen the play spirit as tutelary
deity, though we often give it a more high-toned name. We are
pursuing inquiry, we say, "for its own sake." The history of education can be schematically but not inaccurately summarized as
the effort by educational philosophers to maximize one of these
modes and obelize the other two. The Progressive movement put
all its eggs in the play basket; advocates of professional teaching
today, and of the old nineteenth-century moral gymnasium curricula, centralized the competition motive; the history of "practical" education has taken purposive motivation as its referent.
Seldom does an educational philosopher urge a radical *mixture*
of motives as the ideal situation. Whitehead's *Aims of Education*,
for example, pleads this case, but there are few books like it. It
is so much easier to concentrate on one orienting variable.

Especially when you invent legitimating premises for research.
The practical-purpose motive is shunted to one side—into engineering on the scientific side, into schools of education, and into
composition on the humanities side. We are left in the humanities
and, to narrow our focus, in English studies, with play—"for its
own sake"—as the recognized motive and competition as the
back-room compulsion. English departments have charted their
central pattern of inquiry by orienting themselves around the play
motive, and it is that motive that has come to maturity now. This
maturity brings its dangers, just as maximizing either of the other
variables does: the play motive in its pure form leads to anti-
quarian diddling; the competition motive to the "paper chase"
kind of educational pathology; the practical motive to what C.
Wright Mills used to call "crackpot practicality," a blind concen-
tration on immediate use to the detriment of long-term purpose.

The great and exciting periods of research have been those when
the three motives worked intensely, and tensely, together. Atomic
physics in the decade surrounding World War II provides perhaps
the best recent instance of this tense mixture. The subject dis-
played the greatest possible theoretical elegance; the competition

took place among a small group of geniuses who played off against each other, the personal competition spiced, during the war, by racing Germany for the bomb; and, for practical purpose, there was the fission reaction itself—the extreme instrument for death or the ultimate energy for life. The theory was galvanized and the competition purified by the practical dangers of what Whitehead called the "insistent present." Atomic physics does not provide the only example, of course. If I had the time I might cite the history of microbiology research from the early days of the phage group to the discovery of the DNA double helix. There the same rich mixture of motives enlivened the proceedings at every turn. But in all such instances the structural principle remains constant: in research, both excitement and results come not from the purity of one's motives but from a radical impurity, a dynamic mixture.

If we ask where English studies stands now in this spectrum of motive mixing, we shall get different answers. If English studies today is suffused by the same excitement that accompanied Niels Bohr's Institute for Theoretical Physics in Copenhagen or that electrified Watson and Crick's laboratory at the Cavendish, then literature ought to be left alone, to have nothing to do with composition. If, however, English studies stands at the end of an exhausted paradigm, if it is becoming trivialized by hypertrophy of the play motive and acidified by hyperintense competition, then the teaching and study of composition appear in a new light. They offer not a burden but an opportunity. They have to offer exactly what literary studies needs—a big problem, an insistent present. The kind of problem that mixes your motives for you.

Three

Here we pass from questions one and two to question three, the relation between the two ways to ask the question, the theoretical and the practical. For if you subscribe to the problem as I have just presented it, composition practice can redeem and enrich literary theory. The great power of the literacy crisis comes out of the enormousness of its problem. Research is redeemed by big problems. Big problems are what research is for. The more abstruse the theory, the more it needs a big problem. This is why big second-level university campuses are potentially so much better placed for English studies in the next decade than the reigning aristocrats. *They know the problem in their bones*. They live with it as the context of their literary thinking. *Nocte dieque incubando.* That context changes how literary thinking is done. I think it is going to change it for the better.

The literacy crisis presents literary studies with an enormous problem. We can of course ignore it, draw our wagons into a circle, and hope for the best. But if we do this, I think that sooner or later the problem will kill us. If we try instead to solve the crisis, dangerous as the trying will be, we may find that the crisis has redeemed us, both our teaching and our research—put literary study back in the center of modern humanism where in our hearts we know it belongs. It may very well be that "the gulfs will wash us down," but who knows? Perhaps we will return to the roots of our literary heritage, "touch the Happy Isles / And see the great Achilles, whom we knew."

2   The Humor of Composition
Josephine Miles

Who thinks literature can work without a sense of workability
or that composition can compose without a sense of literary powers? Don't readers need to write and writers read? Despite all the
debates on language today, despite the debates on literature and
composition, these reciprocities need to be assumed. As we work
by habits and expectations, so we participate not only in others'
reading and writing processes but also in our own.

The so-called gaps are interesting. Ignoring the terrible truth
that they may mean merely the contrast between appreciating
good stuff and criticizing bad stuff (marking all misspellings and
typos), we may note that gaps have something to do with differences in expectations. Are we awaiting the upshot of *Walden* or
of my summer vacation? But even in such differences rests the
bridge over the gaps of complexity, that is, the functioning of
basic sentence structures. What we expect from Thoreau we can
expect from ourselves too—good strong composing of sentences
into ideas.

If we look closely at basic sentence structures, we can easily
recognize the common working base. And one way to look closely
is to examine the structures of a special compositional form, the
joke, wherein the point is based on the disruption of standard
expectations.

The working parts of sentences are so charming in their subject-
predicate-modifier configurations that I can never be patient with
the best-selling textbooks that cut down the subject, break down
the subject, outline the subject, diminish the modifiers, and let
the verb function somewhere in right field outside the outline.
Rather, I think we know, it is the predicate that needs organizing,
and nothing needs breaking down if the steps presented by the
verb are clear.

The traditional place-time-manner of civic guidelines allows for
topos, or placing, but not for cutting in pieces; rather, for locating

the procedures of the verb in the grammar of coherent statement, the logic of verifiable statement, the rhetoric of effective statement. It's in the links that the structures are achieved, and it's in the links that the structures may become jokes—that is, in violation of due process, "an element in a situation that acts in an unexpected way."

If we see how jokes act unexpectedly, we may better see how regular sentence structures act expectedly. Let me first call to mind some familiar and admired expected structures, standard or more than standard, then turn to the humor of some unexpected ones. In a time when patterning is so important to word processing, we are fortunate to be reminded by our jokesters of the very fundamentals we need to recognize.

The rain in Spain stays mainly in the plain.

This statement composes language. It composes letters, syllables, and grammatical units.

The grammatical units it composes are the verb *stays,* which it applies to the subject *rain,* plus three modifiers, one for the subject—*in Spain*—and two for the verb *mainly* and *in the plain,* spelling out how and where.

The literary or artistic quality of the statement is enhanced by further compositional patterning, as by the alliteration and rhyme, used for tonal effect—in this case a heavy repetition that seems to lead to absurdity.

Saying something about something is making a connection, making a text. The pre*dic*ate, from *dic* ("to say"), says something about the *sub*(under)*ject*(put). Preachers, for example, choose texts to develop for their sermons. Teachers write texts to carry ideas about information. The text works between giver and receiver and operates well, if some shared effects are managed, toward what is called understanding. Why worry then about who speaks or writes the text, whether Shakespeare or one of us? Because at times so much fuller effect is achieved by one of us than by another. So how improve? How succeed? We are told to write or speak "clearly," "simply"; well-known authors like George Orwell and E. B. White tell us many errors not to make. But errors can be trifling. Whole positive structures are essential to following how texts work.

Abraham Lincoln began his famous Gettysburg Address, which he was at first not very happy with, as follows: "Four score and seven years ago our fathers brought forth on this continent, a new nation, conceived in Liberty, and dedicated to the proposition that all men are created equal.''

A fine sentence for a beginning writer to look at, to begin with! Why? Because it's simple and clear all right, and because, in addition, it's complex and puzzling; it says more than we can quickly receive and much that we can spend a long time thinking about.

What is the central sentence? *Our fathers brought forth a nation.* And how is the statement modified? First by a phrase of time, *fourscore and seven years ago,* then by a phrase of place, *on this continent,* then by the simple adjective *new,* then by two modifying phrases, *conceived* with its phrase, and *dedicated* with its phrase and resounding clause, *that all men are created equal.* With such a sentence ringing in one's ears, how could one write some sort of ill-adjusted confusion? Unless one were confused, of course, and that's the happy story: good sentences, tried out on the ear, can help unconfuse one. And practicing is a way of trying them out.

So we need to recognize and use the working parts of predicate and subject with their modifiers. The *rain stays* on the plain. Or, A good *man is* hard to find. Or, Now *we are engaged* in a great civil war. The verb of the predicate provides the structure of further development. This is what we outline, not the subject, that is inert. The modifiers, whether words, phrases, or clauses, provide the specification that will make the statement verifiably true or false. So the grammar sets up clear expectations for the reader to be led by. In grammar is the power to clarify and develop statements. Think of how Bertrand Russell begins an idea, setting up the steps of development: "In arriving at a scientific law there are three main stages: the first consists in observing the significant facts; the second in arriving at a hypothesis, that, if it is true, would account for these facts; the third in deducing from this hypothesis consequences which can be tested by observation." Or how Gibbon casts his net wide in sweeping statement: "The greatness of Rome . . . was founded on the rare and almost incredible alliance of virtue and of fortune." Large subject, weightily modified predicate, resting on powerful substantives to be demonstrated.

To be able to recognize such purposeful composition of elements is to understand how literature works, how arrangement carries tone. Say one is wearing formal dress with tennis shoes; the combination calls for an explanation—perhaps of error, perhaps of satire, perhaps of differing expectations. So too with the components of language. Gibbon sets up expectations for a large sweep of generalization; Russell, for categories of thought; Lincoln, for the significant pressures of the moment.

I propose that one good way to understand the parts and wholes of literary composition is to think about jokes. The point of a joke is that it *mis*leads. Therefore we can follow the leads of composition through the ways of jokes and riddles to mislead. For example, the riddle, *Why does a chicken cross the road?* Or, *Why does a fireman wear red suspenders?* The beginning with a specific subject, *a* chicken or *a* fireman, makes us think that a predicate that is true of these specifically will follow; what are the special qualities of chickens or firemen that will help in the answer? But then the joke is in the slippage to a more general predicate: Why does *anyone* cross the road or wear suspenders? The hearer feels foolish because he has been taking the subject too seriously and not simply thinking about the basic question in the predicate.

An opposite mistake in attention is possible too. Not only may the speaker seem to emphasize the subject, as, for example, the *Encyclopaedia Britannica* does by definition, he may also seem to stress the predicate, with surprising results. So when in *Endgame* the son rebelliously cries out to his father, "Oh, why did you ever conceive me?" the father miserably answers, "Because I didn't realize it would be you." The whole meaning of the *why* predicate shifts its weight from the verb *conceive* to the subject *you* in devastating fashion.

In straight composition this would be an error, a confusion; in joke composition it is a collapse or skid from one series of expectations to another, very like a stock pratfall, slipping on a banana peel, a landing different from the one expected.

Jokes play across grammar. Grammar sets up the clearest expectations we have for statement making, and jokes capitalize upon those expectations by working within the rules but using them in their other potentialities. In addition to the selection of basic subject and predicate, let's consider the modifiers also— their subtle tricks, and how they need careful composing toward their purpose. For example (note that these jokes are taken from a family magazine):

A man whose son is named for him says that the other day
his wife answered the phone and a childish voice asked,
"May I speak to Harry?"

"Do you want big Harry or little Harry?"

"Uh, big Harry, I guess," replied the voice. "The one in the
fourth grade."

Note how expectations for *little* Harry are carefully developed in
the selection of husband and wife and then child's voice, the wife's
carefully and naturally constructed question and the child's equally
careful answer, specifying *fourth grade,* big from such a special
perspective.

In another example, a verb *carry* becomes an adverb, *fast,* to
good humorous deflating effect:

"Is it true," the reporter asked the famous explorer, "that
wild animals in the jungle won't harm you if you carry a
torch?"

"That depends," said the explorer, "on how fast you carry
it."

Or a lot of superlative adjectives are shifted to one simple
comparative:

James Thurber and a friend attended the opening of a play
that proved to be a bore from beginning to end. As they left
the theater, the friend said, "That was the dullest, dreariest,
and shoddiest play I ever saw."

This off his chest, he continued, "And what did you think of
it?"

"Well," said the humorist, "I didn't think it was that good."

The report rests on the evaluating adjectives applied to the play
by Thurber's friend. The shift rests on Thurber's use of a predicate, a verb, and an intensive adverb instead of the negative
adjectives.

Note such a shift also from *rash* to *again,* from intense interest
in the noun, to a letdown in an adverb.

Not being able to identify his patient's green rash, the doctor
asked, "Have you had this trouble before?"

"Yes," was the reply.

"Well, you have it again," the doctor said.

A similar and tremendous shift from adjective *sober* to adverb *today:*

> The driller wrote on the daily log: "Derrick man was drunk today."
>
> After sobering up, the derrick man pleaded with him to strike it out of the record. "It's the first time in my life I've been drunk," he said, "and I promise I'll never do it again."
>
> "In this log we write only the truth," said the driller.
>
> At the end of the following day, the derrick man scrawled at the bottom of the log, "Driller was sober today."

Sometimes the modifiers may be not merely single words but whole phrases or clauses, as in the play on logic in the *if* clauses of Churchill and Lady Astor:

> After one hot and heavy interchange in Parliament, Lady Astor is reported to have said to Churchill, "Winston, if you were my husband, I'd poison your coffee."
>
> "If you were my wife, Nancy," replied Churchill suavely, "I'd drink it."

The parallel of clauses and then the contrast of *husband* to *wife* sharpen the point of logic.

The shift from the noun *superstition* to the verb in the clause *whether* in this joke is another example:

> A reporter interviewing a noted scientist noticed that he was wearing a rabbit's foot on his key chain.
>
> "Surely," said the reporter, "you, a man of science, don't believe in that old superstition."
>
> "Certainly not," said the scientist, "but a friend of mine tells me it's supposed to bring you luck whether you believe in it or not."

A simple joke or "yoke" (a pun is another sort of joke) on *confidence* says it is "that quiet feeling of assurance you have just before you fall on your face." The static adjective *quiet* serves in contrast to the active verb.

As we have seen, not only the grammar of language but also its logic and rhetoric can be illuminated by the gaps, the intended slips, of literary composition—for example, the odd logic of *but,* in "Abstinence is a good thing, but it should always be practiced in moderation." The three basic logical constructions—additive, alternative, and implicative—with their negatives, can all be played upon, as in Churchill's *if,* already quoted, and this comparative:

"What is the difference between results and consequences?" the teacher asked a bright student.

Responded the youngster, "Results are what you expect, consequences are what you get."

In rhetoric—the stress or tonal effect—it is again perspective that shifts, especially the contrast of general to particular, or normative to descriptive, that comes into play—the "out in the West where men are *men*" sort of phrasing, where both uses of a word, its neutral and its loaded, highlight the sequence. In a joke, the highlighting may well be in reverse, as in the idealistic but then actual *help* of the Boy Scouts, where ideally considered *help* as a good term becomes negative in shifted perspective:

Scoutmaster: "Yes, of course helping an old lady across the street counts as a good deed for the day. I'm wondering why it took three of you."

Scout: "Well, it wasn't easy. She didn't want to go."

Or Gilbert Lewis's "Do you believe in baptism?" "Believe in it?—I've seen it done!" Or the simple "I don't want to want what I want." Or:

"My wife has a terrible memory."

"Forgets everything?"

"No. She remembers."

There is a good shift from neutral to pejorative in the kinder-gartner's use of *call:*

The kindergarten teacher asked a new arrival what her father's name was.

"Daddy," replied the girl.

"No, I mean his first name—What does your mother call him?"

"She doesn't call him anything," said the little one. "She likes him."

Nobody recommends analyzing a joke. I don't always recommend analyzing grammar either. I'd prefer the simple feeling for humor like the simple feeling for language that comes from that quiet feeling of confidence already mocked. Awareness of custom, awareness of cliché, awareness of literature, awareness of our assumptions, all help us keep in balance and avoid slipping on the too obvious banana peel. What is it we want to know about composition in letters, in language? How to pull our thoughts together, how to follow the thoughts of others, how to substantiate general truths and generalize specific ones. How to discriminate between safe and precarious footing in the field of words, and so proceed with true confidence in both the reading of literature and the writing of composition. The writer who amalgamates from encyclopedia styles, the writer who talks about outlining the subject, or the writer who launches forth on a topic without the carrying force of an idea—all need to recover from their struggling over the gaps and see them rather as synapses, the predicative energies carrying across the units of letter and phrase, of grammar, logic, and rhetoric, of reading and writing, of literature and composition to arrive safely where they intend to go.

3 Composition and Decomposition
Deconstruction and
the Teaching of Writing

J. Hillis Miller

My topic is the relation between writing and reading, or between the teaching of writing and the teaching of reading. In what ways do they, or might they, facilitate one another or inhibit one another? The title of this essay might have been "Rhetoric and Rhetoric," or "The Trivium: Where Three Roads Cross," the latter with a memory that it was at such a triple fork that Oedipus killed Laius. Is one rhetoric, rhetoric as analysis, the study of tropes, the oedipal murderer of the other rhetoric, rhetoric as persuasion, as synthesis, as the effective composition of essays or the composition of effective essays, writing with a purpose? The trivium, in medieval education, comprised grammar, logic, and rhetoric. It was preliminary or propaedeutic to the quadrivium: arithmetic, geometry, astronomy, and music, the finishing touches to a liberal arts education. The seven form a sequence. It is impossible to go on to the second group until you have mastered the first, though the image of the three meeting roads suggests that the elements of the trivium are somehow inextricably connected, as in turn are those of the quadrivium, where four roads cross. In any case, if students come to college these days not knowing grammar, we must begin there before we can go on to logic or dialectic and then to rhetoric, much less hope to attain to harmony and the music of the spheres.

It might seem that from the point of view of either pedagogy it would be better for each to go it alone. The teaching of writing, it might be said, has established itself anew as an important separate discipline, with its independent institutionalization in the form of professional societies, meetings, journals, a hierarchy of distinguished practitioners, and so on. This new or reborn discipline has a double strength. It founds itself on the most advanced twentieth-century scientific or quasi-scientific discoveries about the nature of language and the nature of composition, the processes whereby writing is generated and revised. In addition it has the most urgent practical necessity and pragmatic grounding: daily contact with writing samples from thousands of students. The emphasis can happily be on *praxis* as opposed to *theoria*. Such theory as there is is immediately testable in practice. The discipline is required to appropriate only as much theory as it needs and as works, while ideas can fairly easily and quickly be shown not to work and can be hooted out of court. When one adds to this the strong public and institutional support for the teaching of writing, one has what seem almost ideal conditions for the flourishing of an independent discipline. It is not surprising that just this is happening in many places. Independent departments or programs in composition are beginning to overshadow the adjacent departments of English literature in size, strength, and funding.

By contrast, programs in literature seem, in some colleges and universities at least, increasingly marginal and detached from present conditions. Their enrollments and numbers of majors are declining. Peter Demetz, in a recent essay based on his experience as president of the Modern Language Association and as chairman of the MLA Commission on the Future of the Profession, reports that from 1969 to 1979 the number of college freshmen choosing to major in English declined from 6.1 percent of the women and 1.1 percent of the men to 1.2 percent of the women and 0.6 percent of the men. Demetz cites a report of the National Council on Education predicting that by 1986–87 the percentage of B.A.s in English and American literature will reach a low of 2.7 percent of all degrees awarded.[1] By contrast, of course, programs in writing have proliferated and are flourishing even where, as at Yale, there is no "writing requirement." Teachers of English literature seem to have been relatively less able than teachers of composition to accommodate themselves to current social, economic, and ideological realities. Teachers of literature may either remain stubbornly stuck in traditional canons and methods of teaching or allow themselves to become victims of the merely fashionable and often spuriously "relevant" in the attempt to attract students. Moreover, these days departments of English literature are often

1. Peter Demetz, "An Inarticulate Society," *Yale Alumni Magazine and Journal* 45, no. 2 (November 1981): 16, and see also "Recommendations of the Commission on the Future of the Profession," in *Profession 81* (New York: Modern Language Association, 1981), 1–5, especially recommendation 3, to which this present book may be said to be a response.

the locus of rarefied battles among competing theories of criticism, mostly foreign imports—Lacanian psychoanalysis, structuralism, semiotic Marxism, phenomenology, so-called deconstruction, and so on. These may seem to have almost nothing to do with the practical business of teaching English literature, much less with teaching English composition. Many or even most of the teachers of literature in such departments are in any case indifferent or downright hostile to these theories and seek to minimize their influence. Teachers of composition would seem to do well to leave the literary theorists to their monastic disputes and the departments of English to the general disarray or glum conservatism of their enterprise.

On the other hand, it is not altogether clear that theory can so blithely be separated from practice. Their relation is a complex one—neither safe separation, nor smooth transition, nor easy overlapping or meshing. It seems that the teaching of composition is primarily a practical matter. Writing well is learned gradually as an acquired habit, like speech itself. On the other hand, composition handbooks are full of theoretical statements, not only about language, but also about the ethical, ideological, and even political matters that are inextricably connected with assumptions about language. Even the most immediate practical advice to a student about his writing has such implications. Such advice or instruction is not innocent. It is not evident that it is good either for the student or for the teacher to remain innocent of this lack of innocence. It is not clear, either, that *praxis* can, in any case, really be taught in detachment from the *theoria* it presupposes, unless we think students can learn to write blindly, by rote, whereas it appears our aim should be to teach them to use language freely as a means to some end, to write effectively and for a purpose. Most teachers of composition no doubt find themselves again and again in the somewhat embarrassing situation of teaching not just grammar and rhetoric but also logic, ethics, politics, even something of theology and the music of the spheres.

At the other extreme, even those rarefied debates about literary theory have practical implications for the teaching not just of reading but of writing. Such debates have their correlates in the day-to-day practices of writing and the teaching of writing. Much might be gained by trying to bring these correlations into the open. As Paul de Man put this in a recent essay, if "the disputes among literary theorists more and more appear to be like quarrels among theologians, at the furthest remove from any reality or practicality," at the same time "disputes among theologians, for all their abstruseness, have in fact very public equivalents: how is one to separate the disputations between nominalists and realists in the fourteenth century from 'the waning of the Middle Ages?' " In the same way, the "nearly imperceptible line" between a semiotician and grammarian of poetry like Michael Riffaterre and a theoretician of rhetoric like de Man may, as de Man says, "be inextricably intertwined with the 'waning' of modernity."[2] That is to say, it may be closely associated with the social and ideological situation within which the teaching of writing takes place today. If this is the case, anything that can be done to effect a rapprochement between literary theory and the teaching of writing would be all to the good. The theorists of literature would do well to face the practical implications for the teaching of writing as well as of the teaching of reading of their theories, and the teachers of writing would do well to be as clear as possible about the theoretical assumptions of what they do.

This makes a strong argument for not detaching programs in composition from departments of English. The teaching of reading and the teaching of writing must go hand in hand. Writing disabilities are no doubt evidence of corresponding reading disabilities, and the latter may be even harder to detect and remedy. Failures in grammar or idiom are there on the page of a writing sample, relatively easy to spot if not to help the student correct, while the strange things that may go on in a student's mind when he reads a page of Milton, of Jane Austen, or of Stevens, not to speak of the newspaper or of a textbook in political science, are more difficult to bring into the open, much less ameliorate.

Nevertheless, reading is itself a kind of writing, or writing is a trope for the act of reading. Every act of writing is an act of reading, an interpretation of some part of the totality of what is. That totality is not a set of nonlinguistic objects but a field of signs to be read, which means to have more signs added to them by the new composition. If reading and writing are so intimately connected, the teachers of writing have as much to gain from making sure their colleagues in literature have taught students the rudiments of reading (if only we were sure these days what that might mean) as the teachers of literature have to gain from having

2. Paul de Man, "Hypogram and Inscription: Michael Riffaterre's Poetics of Reading," forthcoming in *Diacritics*.

42 J. Hillis Miller

the art of writing correctly and persuasively well taught (assuming we know what that might mean). As a matter of fact, much of the actual teaching of reading goes on in courses in composition. In any case, any artificial detachment of one from the other will be a disaster for both disciplines.[3]

In spite of these associations, reading and writing seem in many ways to be antithetical activities, as their names suggest. Writing is composition, putting words together in the right order so they will produce a certain effect on the reader or accomplish a certain end. This is rhetoric as persuasion. It works by synthesis. Reading, on the other hand, is decomposition, deconstruction, the analysis or untying of the links that bind a piece of language together so that the reader can see how it works and make sure he has grasped its meaning correctly. The act of reading well seems, then, to go in the opposite direction from the act of writing well. Reading is not rhetoric as putting together, composition, but rhetoric as taking apart, the study of tropes, decomposition. It is easy to see, however, that no skillful composition is possible without that prior act of decomposition practiced through reading models of composition by others. I learn to make a chair by studying the way another man has made a chair, and this probably means taking his handiwork apart to see in detail how he did it. There is no learning to write well without a concomitant learning to read well. There is no help for it. Those involved in programs in writing either must make sure that reading is being well taught by their colleagues in literature or must teach reading themselves. Of what would good teaching of reading consist?

Among the most powerful and challenging techniques of reading today is the one called "deconstruction." Sentences of the form "Deconstruction is so and so" are a contradiction in terms. Deconstruction cannot by definition be defined, since it presupposes the indefinability or, more properly, "undecidability" of all conceptual or generalizing terms. Deconstruction, like any method of interpretation, can only be exemplified, and the examples will of course all differ. By deconstruction I mean reading as it is practiced by Jacques Derrida, Paul de Man, and myself, along

3. I am glad to find support for this belief not only in the third recommendation of the MLA Commission, referred to in note 1 above, but also in an accompanying essay by Wayne Booth, "The Common Aims That Divide Us: Or, Is There a 'Profession 1981'?" in *Profession 81*, 13–17.

with an increasing number of others in this country and abroad.[4]
A large number of teachers and critics are pursuing the renewal
of this rhetoric of reading along parallel but not always convergent
or superposable lines. A new undergraduate major at Yale, the
literature major, is devoted, in part at least, to developing a reading and writing curriculum from freshman and sophomore courses
on up to introduce students to the renewed development of a
rhetorical analysis of texts. Other colleges and universities are
developing similar programs. I speak of deconstruction as if it
were one special technique of reading, but in fact deconstruction
is a currently fashionable or notorious name for good reading as
such. All good readers are and always have been deconstructionists.

To take a little further my claim that the two forms of rhetoric,
rhetoric as persuasion and rhetoric as knowledge of tropes, have
always gone hand in hand, along with my argument that all good
readers are deconstructionists, I must mildly take issue with an
assertion made by Winifred Horner in her admirable introduction
to this volume. She says that there was in the eighteenth century
"a shift in emphasis in the general thrust of language study from
the creative act to the interpretative act." Broadly speaking, this
seems a fair sketch of the history of rhetoric, but the double or
bifurcated definition of rhetoric of course goes back to the Greeks.
As Horner herself observes, the taxonomy of tropes is almost all
the work of the Greeks. Our "proper" English words for the
various figures of speech—metaphor, metonymy, hyperbole, irony,
apostrophe, prosopopoia, parable, parabasis, and the rest—are
still the Greek ones. This has a profound historical and linguistic
significance, as does the fact that all the proper names for the
tropes are themselves tropes, though there is not space here to
discuss the latter fact in detail. The eighteenth-century Scottish
development of rhetoric as the study of reading and of tropes was,
like the Renaissance English one with Puttenham and others,
more a revival of a Greek discipline than an innovation. Moving

4. Though a large part of the work of Derrida and de Man would be relevant
to the topic of the rhetoric of reading, two works are especially important, Derrida's "White Mythology: Metaphor in the Text of Philosophy," trans. F. C. T.
Moore, *New Literary History* 6, no. 1 (autumn 1974): 6–74, originally "La my-
thologie blanche (la métaphore dans le texte philosophique)," *Poetique*, no. 5
(1971): 1–52, reprinted in *Marges* (Paris: Editions de Minuit, 1972), 247–324; and
de Man's *Allegories of Reading: Figural Language in Rousseau, Nietzsche, Rilke,
and Proust* (New Haven and London: Yale University Press, 1979).

to the renewal of tropological study in our century, one can say
that it is not an accident that Friedrich Nietzsche, one of the
founding fathers of the modern version of rhetoric as the study
of tropes, was a classical philologist. Nietzsche offered in the
winter term of 1872–73 at Basel a course on classical rhetoric,
not as the art of persuasion but as the taxonomy of figures of
speech.[5] Here, as in so many other areas of thought, the Greeks
had names for it, plus all the accompanying concepts, and the
best we can hope is to reach back up again to where they had
already been, with perhaps some slight additional tropes, twists,
or turns of our own.

The presence of both forms of rhetoric can already be seen in
Plato and Aristotle. It is true that Plato in the *Gorgias* and in the
Phaedrus, speaking of course through Socrates, seems to consider
rhetoric primarily as the study of means of persuasion, licit or
illicit. Plato attacks rhetoric primarily on the grounds that it is
not an art but a "habitude," a "routine" (*empeiria*), a species of
"flattery" (*kolakeia*), a "semblance of a part of politics."[6] To call
something a semblance (*eidolon*) is about the worst thing Plato
can find to say about it, and calling a rhetorician a semblance
links the rhetorician with the Sophist, who is in *The Sophist* condemned as a semblance of the wise philosopher. The rhetorician
is a mere phantom of the true political orator because his power
of persuasion is not based on genuine knowledge of justice—what
is good for the soul—any more than a cook's concoctions are
based on medical knowledge of what is good for the body. This
seems to put rhetoric firmly on the side of composition and to
define it as a skill in persuasion, a base and baseless skill at that.
But when Plato has Socrates in the *Phaedrus* define a kind of
rhetoric that is a genuine art and not a routine and that must
therefore be guided by true knowledge, he gives as the broadest
definition of that knowledge a gift for division and combination.
If you want to be a true rhetorician, you "must know the truth
about the subject that you speak or write about; that is to say,
you must be able to isolate it in definition, and having so defined
it you must next understand how to divide it into kinds, until you

5. See Friedrich Neitzsche, *Gesammelte Werke* (Munich: Musarion Verlag, 1922),
5:285–319, and Friedrich Nietzsche, "Rhetorique et language," trans. Philippe
Lacoue-Labarthe and Jean-Luc Nancy, *Poetique,* no. 5 (1971): 99–142.

6. *Gorgias,* 462c, 463b, and 463d, trans. W. D. Woodhead, *Plato: The Collected
Dialogues,* ed. Edith Hamilton and Huntington Cairns, Bollingen Series 71
(Princeton: Princeton University Press, 1973), 247, 246.

reach the limit of division."[7] So much for division, which should govern the composition of a good piece of writing or speaking. Combination, on the other hand, is the assertion of resemblance between things unlike or not identical. It includes, in fact, the whole region of tropes. Plato (or Socrates) sees this as primarily a resource of the false rhetorician who seeks to persuade his hearers that the false is true, the true false. Here what is needed is skill at analysis, skill in detecting false resemblances—in short, reading defined as decomposition or demystification, what today is called deconstruction. Plato too is a deconstructionist before the fact, and his discussion of rhetoric in the *Phaedrus* contains a program for the study of both kinds of rhetoric.

The same may be said for Aristotle. The basic resources of rhetorical or argumentative persuasion are in Aristotle's *Rhetoric* said to be the example and the enthymeme. The example is a truncated form of inductive logic, the enthymeme, of deductive logic. Both in fact are tropes, figures of speech. Example is a synecdoche, part for whole and then applied to another part, with all the problems belonging to that trope, and the enthymeme is defined as an incomplete syllogism, that is, once more argument by similitude or trope, since the syllogism is a formally stated proportional metaphor.[8]

I turn now to a much later example of how inextricably involved in one another the two kinds of rhetoric are. In a well-known passage in *Middlemarch,* George Eliot observes that "we all of us, grave or light, get our thoughts entangled in metaphors, and act fatally on the strength of them" (book 1, chap. 10). "Entangled": it is of course itself a metaphor, and so an example of what the sentence affirms. Somewhat less well known is a wonderfully witty and penetrating passage in *The Mill on the Floss* (book 2, chap. 1) about poor Tom Tulliver's sufferings in school at the hands of Mr. Stelling. The passage has to do with an example of the general doctrine about metaphor enunciated later in *Middlemarch*. It is an example especially appropriate here, since it has to do with the way fatal errors in pedagogical theory are the result of committing the aboriginal linguistic error of taking a figure of

7. *Phaedrus,* 277b, trans. R. Hackforth, *Collected Dialogues,* p. 522.
8. *Rhetoric,* 1356b, trans. Lane Cooper (New York and London: D. Appleton-Century, 1932), p. 10, and see also *Rhetoric,* 1395b ff., pp. 154 ff.; on proportional metaphor see Aristotle, *On the Art of Poetry,* 1457b, trans. S. H. Butcher (Indianapolis: Bobbs-Merrill, 1975), p. 28.

speech literally. In this case the figure is the one saying the mind is like a field that needs to be plowed and harrowed by grammar and geometry. This metaphor has been preceded by one describing teaching as "instilling" information into the mind of the student. It is followed by three others, that of the mind as an intellectual stomach, and those of the mind as a blank sheet of paper and as a mirror. As George Eliot's narrator ironically exclaims: "It is astonishing what a different result one gets by changing the metaphor!"

A full reading of this admirable text would take up far more space than I have. The passage is a miniature treatise on rhetoric as reading, as well as a little anthology of the basic tropes of the Western tradition. It speaks of the activity of reading, manifests a model of that activity, and invites us to read it according to the method it employs. In all these ways it is exemplary of that form of reading I am calling "deconstructive," or of reading as such. Though good reading does not occur as often as one might expect or hope, it is by no means confined to any one historical period and may appear at any time, perhaps most often in those readers, like George Eliot, who are also good writers, masters of composition. The deconstructive movement of the passage in question is constituted by proffering and withdrawing one metaphorical formulation after another. Each metaphor is dismantled as soon as it is proposed, though the sad necessity of using metaphors is at the same time affirmed.

Far from suggesting that metaphor may be opposed to literal or to conceptual language as an external adornment that might be removed, leaving the naked literal names or concepts, George Eliot sees metaphor as unfortunately an intrinsic part of language. It is not by any means to be stripped away from any discourse or argument, even the most unadorned. The only cure for metaphor is another metaphor, but that new metaphor only inoculates you with a somewhat different disease. As George Eliot says of this lamentable linguistic predicament: "It was doubtless an ingenious idea to call the camel the ship of the desert, but it would hardly lead one far in training that useful beast. O Aristotle! if you had had the advantage of being the 'freshest modern' instead of the greatest ancient, would you not have mingled your praise of metaphorical speech as a sign of high intelligence, with a lamentation that intelligence so rarely shows itself in speech without metaphor—that we can so seldom declare what a thing is, except by saying it is something else?"[9]

The camel as ship of the desert is not just an example of metaphor. It is a metaphor of metaphor, that is of transfer or transport from one place to another. This is not only what the word "metaphor" etymologically means, but also what metaphor does. If Puttenham's far-fetched Renaissance name for metalepsis is "the Far-fetcher," he calls metaphor the "Figure of Transport." Metaphor gets the writer or reader from here to there in his argument, whether by that "smooth gradation or gentle transition to some other kindred quality" of which Wordsworth speaks in *Essays upon Epitaphs*,[10] echoing the Socrates of the *Phaedrus* on "shifting your ground little by little,"[11] or by the sudden leap over a vacant place in the argument of which George Meredith writes: "It is the excelling merit of similes and metaphors to spring us to vault over gaps and thickets and dreary places."[12] Pedagogy is metaphor. It takes the mind of the student and transforms it, transfers it, translates it, ferries it from here to there. A method of teaching, such as Mr. Stelling's, is as much a means of transportation as a camel or a ship. My own "passages" from Plato and Eliot are synecdoches, parts taken from large wholes and used as figurative means of passage from one place to another in my argument.

The sentence about the camel brings into the open the asymmetrical juxtaposition between the opposition of literal and figurative language, on the one hand, and the opposition of practice and theory on the other. The reader may be inclined to think they are parallel, but this probably depends on a confusion of mind. One thinks of literal language as the clear, nonfigurative expression of ideas or concepts, for example, "the abstract" concepts of grammar, such as the relation between cases and terminations in the genitive or the dative that Tom Tulliver has so much trouble learning, just as a modern student of English composition has trouble learning the rules of English grammar. At the same time

9. See Aristotle, *On the Art of Poetry*, 1458b, p. 31: "But the greatest thing by far is to have a command of metaphor. This alone cannot be imparted by another; it is the mark of genius."

10. William Wordsworth, *The Prose Works,* ed. W. J. B. Owen and J. W. Smyser (Oxford: Clarendon Press, 1974), 2:81.

11. *Phaedrus,* 262a, p. 507.

12. George Meredith, *One of Our Conquerors* (New York: C. Scribner's Sons, 1906), chap. 18.

one thinks of literal language as the act of nonfigurative nomi-
nation, calling a spade a spade and a camel a camel, not a ship.
We tend to think of figure as being applied at either end of the
scale from abstract to concrete as an additional ornament making
the literal expression "clear," more "vivid," or more "forceful."
As George Eliot's sentence makes "clear," however, the trouble
with theory is not that it is abstract or conceptual but that it is
always based on metaphor—that is, it commits what Alfred North
Whitehead calls the "fallacy of misplaced concreteness."

If it is true, as both Whitehead himself and such literary theorists as William Empson and Kenneth Burke aver in different
ways, that original thinking is most often started by a metaphor,
it is also the case that each metaphorically based theory, such as
the alternative pedagogical theories George Eliot sketches out,
has its own built-in fallacious bias and leads to its own special
form of catastrophe in the classroom. If a camel is not a ship, the
brain is neither a field to plow nor a stomach nor a sheet of paper
nor a mirror, though each of these metaphors could, and has,
generated ponderous, solemn, and intellectually cogent theories
of teaching. Neither theory nor literal meaning, if there is such a
thing (which there is not), will help you with that camel. As soon
as you try to tell someone how to manage one you fall into theory—that is, into some metaphorical scheme or other. The opposition between theory and practice is not that between
metaphorical and literal language, but that between language, which
is always figurative through and through, and no language—silent
doing. If the praxis in question is the act of writing, the habit of
writing well, it can be seen that there are going to be problems
in teaching it, more problems even than in teaching someone how
to drive a camel or make a chair. That the terms for the parts of
a chair are examples of those basic personifying catachreses
whereby we humanize the world and project arms and legs where
there are none may cause little trouble as the apprentice learns
from watching the master cabinetmaker at work, but it might
cause much trouble to someone writing about chairs.

The task, most people would agree, is not to teach students in
writing courses grammatical theory, but to make each student
pass somehow from a condition in which he or she cannot write
well to a condition in which he or she can write well. First the
student cannot write well and later he or she can. To make this
happen is perhaps more difficult than to make that camel pass

through a needle's eye. No theoretical metaphor helps much in thinking about this strange transition or carrying over, much less in making it happen. What goes on in the student's mind, whether it is plowed and harrowed, or digests the practical rules of good writing, or has them "instilled" by a process of slow dripping, or is inscribed with them, or reflects them, is in a way irrelevant. It is an adjacent matter of theoretical speculation. What counts is the practical results, the words a given student puts down on paper, and yet what is said to the student or what he reads seems to have something to do with this transition.

So far I have emphasized the insight into the fundamentally figurative character of language in rhetoric as reading, as decomposition, whether that rhetoric is ancient, Victorian, or contemporary deconstructionist. My argument is that if both teachers and students of rhetoric as composition do not aim to become as good readers as Plato, George Eliot, or Derrida, as wise in the ways of tropes, they will not learn to be good teachers or practitioners of writing either. It follows that good courses in rhetoric as reading must always accompany programs in composition, not only in preparation for reading Shakespeare, Milton, Wordsworth, and Wallace Stevens, but as an essential accompaniment to courses in writing. I suspect that the impetus for this new direction in the teaching of reading may come or is coming from the teachers of composition themselves, out of the pressures of their practical encounters with students of writing, but we must make sure we base our rhetoric as reading on the deepest possible knowledge of what good reading would be. Present-day rhetoricians' questioning of reading on the assumption that figures of speech are or should be ornaments added to a literal base of discourse is of course inextricably associated with a set of other questionings: a questioning of the idea that a preexisting, unified self uses language as a tool of expression, writing with a purpose; a questioning of the idea that the writer has his argument clearly in mind first and then copies that mental argument in words, refining it in revision to a closer and closer correspondence to the original;[13] a questioning of the idea that a good piece of writing must or can

13. For a valuable corrective of this paradigm see Nancy Sommers, "Revision Strategies of Student Writers and Experienced Adult Writers," *College Composition and Communication* 35 (1980): 378–88, and for an inside discussion of the relevance of "deconstruction" to the teaching of reading and writing, see Jasper Neel, "Writing about Literature (or Country Ham)," in *Publishing in English Education,* ed. Stephen N. Judy (Montclair, N.J.: Boynton/Cook, 1981).

be "organically unified"; a questioning of the paradigm of "realism" that assumes good writing is to be tested by its correspondence to some external reality. Exploring each of these in its relation to the teaching of both reading and writing would require a separate essay, but the "command of metaphor" in this area too is the key that opens all these doors. Once students of rhetoric in both senses acquire this mastery, all else follows.

On the assumption that this is the case, I shall turn briefly in conclusion to a group of widely used textbooks of composition to see what they have to say about metaphor or figures of speech generally.[14] To analyze the rhetoric and the latent or unthought-out (*impense,* as the French say) ideology of these textbooks, their subtexts, undertexts, or underthoughts, would be a long work. I limit myself to what they say explicitly about metaphor. I have been somewhat surprised by the way most (though not quite all) of them repeat what I should have thought by now would be well-exploded assumptions about the role of figures of speech in good writing. The same figurative terminology for this (the words "vivid" and "concrete" for example) is repeated from textbook to textbook. Or, more precisely, recognition of the constitutive power of figurative language and of the way it is inextricably part of any piece of writing is mingled with many unfortunate vestiges of a set of systematically connected fallacies or received ideas about metaphor. Perpetuating these can in no way help students learn to write. Far from it. Nor can it help students as readers if, for example, they are taught in writing courses to expect metaphor to be a nonessential element in a dialogue of Plato, a novel by George Eliot, or an article in the daily paper.

One of the books I have consulted says nothing at all in any extended way about figures of speech.[15] It is lacking the ritual section present in most handbooks of composition defining met-

14. I have examined the following: Sheridan Baker, *The Complete Stylist and Handbook,* 2d ed. (New York: Harper and Row, 1980); Frederick Crews, *The Random House Handbook,* 3d ed. (New York: Random House, 1980); Elaine P. Maimon, Gerald L. Belcher, Gail W. Hearn, Barbara F. Nodine, and Finbarr W. O'Conner, *Writing in the Arts and Sciences* (Cambridge, Mass.: Winthrop, 1981); James M. McCrimmon, Susan Miller, and Webb Salmon, *Writing with a Purpose,* 7th ed. (Boston: Houghton Mifflin, 1980); Dean Memering and Frank O'Hare, *The Writer's Work: Guide to Effective Composition* (Englewood Cliffs, N.J.: Prentice-Hall, 1980); Robert Scholes and Nancy R. Comley, *The Practice of Writing* (New York: St. Martin's Press, 1981).

15. Scholes and Comley, *Practice of Writing.*

aphor, simile, "dead" metaphor, and "mixed" metaphor and giving hints for their use or avoidance. Perhaps omitting this is a
good thing. At least it does not mislead students by telling them
something mistaken. This strategy has the disadvantage, however,
of suggesting by omission that figurative language is not much of
a problem for the novice writer.

Most other textbooks of composition I have consulted are not
so shy of giving definitions and advice. One book, for example,
though early on it intelligently urges the use of analogy or metaphor as a means of "discovering new ideas about your topic,"
later on takes this back by making what seems to be an extraor-
dinarily odd and unworkable suggestion: "In general, it is best
to avoid metaphor in philosophy papers."[16] Most of the textbooks,
including this one, accept without question the opposition between "abstract ideas," on the one hand, and visible, solid figures
on the other. Metaphor is good because it "makes a picture," is
"clear" or "concrete," and therefore is "fresh" and has "force,"
though all it does is to "illustrate" an idea that remains essentially
the same after its illustration. The idea is only more visible, brought
more into the open, solidified out of its impalpability, like a cement
block. "A figure of speech should be fresh, clear, and should
make an image for the reader," says one book. "The purpose of
the figure of speech is to create a picture, to make an idea clear
and forceful through comparison."[17] "[A] figure of speech," says
another book, "is an effective way to make the abstract concrete.
. . . The analogy . . . pictorializes the argument by likening the
process to something every reader will both understand and feel."[18]

A third book presents a more or less complete repertoire of all
these *idées reçues*:

> [Metaphors are] the most useful way of making our abstrac-
> tions concrete. . . . Metaphors illustrate, in a word, our gen-
> eral ideas. . . . Almost all our words are metaphors, usually
> with the physical picture faded. *Transfer* itself pictures a
> physical portage. . . . But mercifully the physical facts have
> faded—transfer has become a "dead metaphor"—and we can
> use the word in comfortable abstraction. . . . The metaphor,
> then, is your most useful device. It makes your thought con-
> crete and your writing vivid. . . . But it is dangerous. It

16. Maimon et al., *Writing in the Arts and Sciences,* 27, 200–201.
17. Memering and O'Hare, *Writer's Work,* 350.
18. McCrimmon, Miller, and Salmon, *Writing with a Purpose,* 167.

should be quiet, almost unnoticed, with all details agreeing, and all absolutely consistent with the natural universe.[19]

Another textbook, my final example, is the most explicit of those I have consulted in opposing literal to figurative language and in defining metaphor as something optional that may be added after the fact by daring students to a literal discourse existing before any metaphor. The author of this text has a splendid sense of the latent or not so latent comedy in mixed metaphor, but his way of dealing with this is to recommend avoiding metaphor altogether or using it in a wary and deliberate way. His advice reminds me of the creative writing student Mary McCarthy overheard saying she had finished writing her story for the week but "had to go back and put the symbols in":

> Because metaphors and similes usually compress meaning into a minimum of words, they are best attempted after a first draft has given you sufficient control over your *literal* (nonfigurative) meaning. Think of the search for apt images as an optional, potentially fruitful part of the revising process. I say "optional" because some young writers, still engrossed in trying to master principles of effective sentence structure, feel understandably reluctant to carry an extra burden; for a while at least, they can be satisfied if they have weeded out formulaic language and achieved a good measure of concreteness. To insist that they sprinkle their papers with figures of speech would be like asking an intermediate swimming class to concentrate on perfecting the racing turn.
>
> . . . Figurative language, then, is as tricky as it is useful. When you intend an abstract meaning, you have to make sure that your dead metaphors stay good and dead. And when you do wish to be figurative, see whether you are getting the necessary vividness and consistency. If not, go back to the literal statement; it is better to make plain assertions than to litter your verbal landscape with those strangled hulks.[20]

Crews has an interesting account of how he arrived at the figure of the racing turn (after deliberately considering and rejecting three other metaphors).[21] I doubt that this is in fact the way metaphors most commonly get into pieces of writing, good or bad.

19. Baker, *Complete Stylist*, 191, 192, 195.
20. Crews, *Random House Handbook*, 186, 189.
21. Ibid., 186–87.

It would be useful to have broader empirical studies of this, but, lacking these, one may be permitted to guess that the choice of metaphors is usually much more constrained and involuntary, even in those who, like Aristotle's good poet, have that command of metaphor that is the mark of genius. In the passages from Crews I have cited, what about "fruitful," "weeded out," "good measure," "concreteness," "sprinkle," "dead," and that "landscape" "littered" with "strangled hulks"? Were they all the result of clearheaded choice among alternatives? Are they dead metaphors, safely dead; cliché metaphors, tamed, therefore legitimately used without much thought for their consistency with one another (there seems to be some measure of concrete in that weedy garden); mixed metaphors; or figures carefully chosen for their force, clarity, concreteness, and so on? Or are they a kind of ironic in-joke for teachers and shrewd students, strangled hulks of mixed metaphors deliberately left littering the landscape of Crews's prose? Since "strangled hulk" is taken from one of Crews's examples of mixed metaphor (p. 188), it seems that the latter may be the case. In any case, the system of mistaken assumptions about metaphor in these various textbooks may be easily identified. This system includes (1) the idea that metaphor is a detachable part of language, something supplemental, adventitious, or external to a given argument, something the argument could do without and still remain the same argument, a matter of free choice, "optional"; (2) the idea that metaphor may be defined by opposition to some presumed literal language, whether "concrete" or "conceptual"; (3) the idea that a metaphor should be primarily "illustrative," that is, that it should function to make ideas that can in fact be expressed accurately without it more "vivid," "clearer," more "concrete," more "compressed," though without of course essentially changing the idea; (4) the assumption that the logic of metaphor is the logic of mimetic realism—that metaphor must "picture" the real physical world accurately and consistently; (5) the notion that there is such a thing as a "dead metaphor," a harmless fossilized remnant of the etymological origin of abstract words, the belief that these dead metaphors can be counted on, if they are handled right, to remain safely dead, and the conviction that they should remain safely dead; (6) the idea that a student should first write his essay out in entirely literal language, free of all metaphorical adornment, and then, if he dares, go back and add appropriate metaphors, though this is really a matter for advanced students, since metaphors are "dangerous" and should be used sparingly—a little pepper goes a long way; (7) the idea that figures of speech generally may be subsumed under the category of metaphor or analogy. Though simile as a special case of metaphor is usually mentioned, and personification is often identified, these handbooks, with rare exceptions, do not think it necessary to say anything about metonymy or synecdoche, much less about irony, metalepsis, catachresis, chiasmus, or any of the other tropes that the new rhetoric of reading has found it necessary to discriminate. Finally, there is (8) the assumption that information or advice about the use of figurative language is in any case a marginal part of the teaching of writing and can be tucked away somewhere in a paragraph or two as a minor subcategory of "diction." As Jacques Derrida has noted in "White Mythology," the tradition of treating metaphor this way in handbooks of rhetoric goes back at least to Aristotle.[22]

It will be apparent from what I have already said about Plato, Aristotle, and George Eliot that I consider these assumptions false to the actual nature of language and therefore an inadequate basis for the teaching of writing. Metaphors are not like the racing turn. They are the universal medium in which the writer—novice, intermediate, and advanced—must learn to swim. The pervasively figurative nature of language is the "destructive element" in which, to borrow Stein's advice in Lord Jim, all writers must "immerse" themselves in order to swim at all. The "dream" into which we are all born is figurative language itself. Within this dream we must live, and those who try to climb out into the open air of nonfigurative language or out of language altogether will surely drown. "Yes!" says Stein. "Very funny this terrible thing is. A man that is born falls into a dream like a man who falls into the sea. If he tries to climb out into the air as inexperienced people endeavour to do, he drowns—nicht wahr? . . . No. I tell you! The way is to the destructive element submit yourself, and with the exertions of your hands and feet in the water make the deep, deep sea keep you up."[23]

The authors of these handbooks, along with most teachers of composition, would no doubt say, truthfully enough, that they know all this already, but that it is impossible, impractical, or

22. "White Mythology," 30 ff.
23. Lord Jim (London: Dent, 1948), chap. 20.

ineffective to try to teach this to beginning college students. Many such students are only marginally literate and may have drastic "writing disabilities," as they say. It would only make things worse to try to explain figurative language to them. As I have already suggested, the relation between theory and practice is by no means straightforward. Any theory is like that dream Stein recommends we should follow and follow again, *"ewig—usque ad finem,"* though it is not clear that every theory rigorously followed would not lead to some catastrophe. There is always an otherness of theory to itself and therefore an incommensurability of theory and any application of it. To put this another way, empirical studies of the relative effectiveness of different theories of teaching writing are not altogether reassuring. They suggest that students will get somewhat better whatever the teacher does, perhaps through sheer *praxis*. One learns to write by writing. On the other hand, I am enough of a believer in the reasonableness of things to suspect that a thoroughly vitiated theory may come in one way or another to inhibit or vitiate practice. To teach students the doctrine about figures I have found in these textbooks is like limiting classes in sex education to tales about the birds and bees or like assuming in teaching young medical students that though the human body is in fact an organism it is simpler and more workable to tell students it is a wind-up mechanism.

Teachers of writing and reading should take heart from the teachers of mathematics, biology, and physics. Far from trying to hide from students the complexities of new developments in these disciplines, they have gone to work to teach the "new math" from grade school on and to develop appropriate introductory courses teaching new discoveries in genetics and nuclear physics. I believe we should all go to work together, teachers of reading and teachers of writing in cooperation, to do something of the same sort for our disciplines. We should take the most advanced insights into language from both sides and attempt to work out commensurate pedagogies. To some degree this is already happening. The present book is one evidence of the widely felt need for such cooperation. What a "deconstructive" textbook of freshman writing would be like I am not sure, though it would certainly have more and different material on figurative language. Probably the term "deconstruction" has in any case outlived its polemical usefulness as a slogan and should be dropped in such a book. The difficulty of writing such a textbook is not an argument against trying to do it, any more than it is in the analogous situations in biology and physics. In any case, insofar as the teaching of composition suggests that the student should write a literal version first and perhaps add metaphors later; insofar as it still assumes that figures are adventitious adornment; insofar as it assumes that the writer has the ideas before he or she writes them down and that revision is a matter of achieving closer and closer approximation to some preexistent model, whether in the mind of the writer or in some preliminary outline; insofar as it assumes that a good piece of writing should be or can be univocal, wholly unified, it still has much to learn from that form of the rhetoric of reading called at the moment, for better or worse, deconstruction. Insofar as teachers of reading still assume that reading is a passive, objective act and not itself another scene of writing; insofar as they assume that reading is a matter of identifying the literal, thematic sense of the text, its representation of some extralinguistic state of affairs; insofar as they think they can go on blithely teaching the great authors in the canon of English literature as though nothing had happened to the basic literacy of college students, they need to learn from the experience of teachers of composition, or at least from that cooperative teaching of writing and reading I have dared to hope for here.

4 "LITCOMP"

Some Rhetoric Addressed to Cryptorhetoricians about a Rhetorical Solution to a Rhetorical Problem

Wayne C. Booth

To argue against separating "comp" from "lit" is easier than to develop and teach courses that counteract our increasingly sharp divisions.[1] The reasons for our current trends run deep, and only the most inviting of programs can offer any hope of reversing those trends. The test of whether our heartfelt pleas will be more than pious lamentations will lie in our ability to organize courses that will challenge the most challenging of all students, the beginners, and thereby invite back into the freshman classroom those who are not there under orders.

Inviting courses cannot be introduced, as matters are run at most colleges, by those who are now assigned to teach composition, or even COMPLIT. They do not now have the power, they cannot now determine course loads or pay scales or promotion schedules; indeed, most of them do not even have a say in what textbooks they are to use. Their lot is in fact often appalling—it is what one well-known critic recently called "the worst scandal in higher education today."[2]

1. As I have recently done in "The Common Aims That Divide Us; or, Is There a 'Profession 1981'?" in *Profession 81* (New York: Modern Language Association, 1981), 13–17.
2. Namely me. See "A cheap, efficient, challenging, sure-fire and obvious device for combatting the major scandal in higher education today," *Writing Program Administration* 5 (1981): 35–39.

The documentation for my charge of scandalous exploitation is easy to come by: just talk to anyone who takes any of the new "composition" jobs opened up by eliminating tenure tracks. This week I received the following letter from one of our graduate students who holds part-time jobs at two institutions. "I have no office, no telephone," she told me, "and at one place I do not even have a place to hang my coat." "I am not a groaner by nature, but I groan when I look at the 90 blue books and 40 term papers on my dining room table. I groan, not because I must grade them all in seven days, nor because they stand between my "75-book exam" and me. I groan because I am a professional, an experienced professional. I have taught composition well for nine years (with some years off to have a family). I have taught four excellent composition courses at two colleges since September; and I have no voice, no rights, no benefits. My two paychecks amount to about one-fourth what it would cost either college to hire me, with

57

I must address instead those who, powerless as they may sometimes feel, in fact have the power to decide how our departments
will allocate their energies, those who can still choose whether
to oppose the Great Widening Gap. To you—that is, to us—I
would make three simple claims about what we do when we fail
to teach beginning students, or when we agree to teach them only
"lit" and not "comp." First, we cheat those who hire us not
knowing what we really stand for. Second, we help to ensure that
our departments (and of course our own classes) will inherit the
least interesting students from the entering classes; what students
find in that first year will be what they believe about the study of
"English." Finally, we deprive ourselves of one of the highest
intellectual rewards offered by our profession. Most of what follows is addressed to the first and third of these claims; the second
shouldn't require much argument.

First, how can we defend to our various publics what is implied
by our present arrangements, the notion that it is far more important for someone to do another book on Skelton, say, than to
teach beginning students how to read and write, and the twin
notion that the latter is flunky work, best done by those who have
least training? And how do we defend the notion that teaching
"literature" is more important than teaching "composition"?
(Since English has no good word for novels, plays, and poems—
"creative writing," "imaginative literature," *"Dichtung,"* "belles
lettres," "poetry," all are misleading—I shall use quotation marks
when I refer to the relatively narrow conception of literature that
informs most "major field" programs in departments of English
"literature" these days.) More aggressively, what might we say
to an intelligent critic who asks why the public should spend vast

---

my experience and training, as a full-time instructor, with benefits. . . . Part-time
does not mean for me part-professional. I want to talk about my teaching. I am
good, I am innovative, I am human. Even when I am required to design a course
in 24 hours I come through with an organized plan. And I am successful. I groan
because I am a part-timer and I have no right to speak. I am specifically excluded
from faculty meetings at one college and only politely informed of meetings at
the other." Later, on the telephone, she informed me that neither college had
given her any orientation when she began, and that neither provides any chance
for composition teachers to discuss their work together. For fuller documentation
of this scandal see Ben W. McClelland, "Part-time Faculty in English Composition:
A WPA Survey," *Writing Program Administration* 5 (1981): 13–20, and Joseph
Gibaldi and J. V. Mirollo, eds., *The Teaching Apprentice Program* (New York:
Modern Language Association, 1981).

sums to hire two increasingly distinct groups, teachers of writing and teachers of "literature," and why the courses taught by the first group should be required, though the teachers are underpaid and underprotected, while the courses of the second group are mainly electives, taught by people who seem to be rewarded strictly in proportion to their distance from the required courses?

We seem to suggest by this practice that what society really needs is not what we want to provide. We may want to answer that if society really knew what it wanted it would want the kind of students we train in our "literature" courses, people who can appreciate George Eliot and Yeats, people who can write well about "literature." We have in fact produced many a "defense of poesie" showing that the advanced study of "literature" is as important as—maybe even more important than—all other studies.[3] We have taught many students to believe that the way to realize our dreams for them is to produce criticism or scholarship about "literature," and that to do anything else, to get "only a job teaching composition," to become a scholar of anything other than "literature," to take a job in government or business—in short, to depart from the paths of pure "literature" leading to the green fields of graduate teaching—is failure.

Our critic might well argue that the way we now order things conveys a highly unfavorable message about who we think we are and why we think we should be supported. If we imply by everything we do that our most honored positions have no real pertinence to what we think all students should learn, why should the critic believe that supporting us will benefit the education she cares for? Might she not want to say that a profession with no better rationale does not deserve to be supported by the public at all?

Since our critic *is* intelligent, she will want to support any kind of education that promises a citizenry who can read, think, and write. But if we tell her that true success in our profession has nothing to do with teaching a "citizenry" anything, but rather is found in teaching an elite how to write to each other about "literature," she may very well do what many corporations are now

3. The best recent one I know is *The Place of Poetry: Two Centuries of an Art in Crisis,* by Christopher Clausen (Lexington: University Press of Kentucky, 1981). The debate about his book, conducted in the *Georgia Review* (winter 1981), makes a good source for the issues raised when we think about the role of "literature" in education and in public life.

doing: instead of supporting college English departments, they are increasingly setting up "English" courses on the job, so that employees may belatedly learn how to speak and write passable English.

If we look honestly at the quality of writing and thinking exhibited by most of the graduates of most of our colleges—and I by no means exclude the "elite" institutions—it is hard not to conclude that they have been cheated. We recruit students with a promise to educate them. We then for the most part offer them training in "major fields" that generally require little writing and cultivate at best one very narrow range of thought: how to think like—or mimic the thinking of—economists; how to think like—or mimic the thinking of—chemists; of mathematicians, of engineers, of business executives. Some specialties do seem to require, by their nature, considerable writing: philosophy, English, history, the social sciences. It is surprising, though, how many even of these manage to deny their nature. And, even at best, major programs in these fields seldom educate graduates who could be expected—let us make the test easy—to address a congressman effectively, in speech or writing, or to write a plausible letter to a school superintendent urging an improved high-school curriculum. What, then, should we be trying for? Our answer must not be in terms of this or that subject matter, and it will not do to list only the *necessary* skills (such as minimal proficiency in spelling or grammar) that are by no means *sufficient*.[4] What we must seek are programs likely to educate bachelors of arts who can read, think, and write in educated ways—B.A.s whose critical capacities will not shame us.

Anyone who dares to offer a sample program in response to that challenge, as I am now going to do, must be aware of the radical inadequacy of any one suggestion in meeting our needs. Our educational situation is unprecedented, for many reasons: we are trying to educate the first generation of children of "TV

4. This is hardly the place for a tirade about the degraded ideas of "English" that we have somehow managed to encourage in the public (after all, practically all of those who make up our public have passed through our courses, or through courses taught by those who passed through our courses). But it is appalling to see what books about "good English" the public makes into best-sellers: effective writing reduced to questions of style, style reduced to questions of spelling and grammar and correct idiom, grammar reduced to the listing of pet peeves like "hopefully" and "different than."

parents"; we are at last in what can be called the computer age; we are trying to give a college education, for the first time in history, to more than half of our population, for many of whom English is—or is like—a second language. None of this means that liberal education is less desirable than it used to be. But it does mean that pressures toward producing minimal "service courses" and teaching the less-than-basics have increased. Those pressures in turn mean that to make our case we must have many different trial programs, addressed to many local situations.

We should, in short, seek to agree not on single models but rather on the capacities we hope will be exhibited by those who encounter our many different models. Before offering my own trial program, then, let me suggest the general practices I have tried to build into it—practices I think will be found in every educational experience that produces graduates who do not shame us. What practices can we say with some certainty *will have been enjoyed* by those graduates who reflect honor on our efforts, whether they majored in English or not? My little list is of course banal: the "basic practices" are by nature not secrets, though a surprising number of administrators seem never to have heard of them.[5]

1. Every such student will have written frequent papers—several papers a month *for several years*. The papers need not be long. Weekly one-pagers can work marvels, even in the later years, provided they are closely read—by *somebody*.

2. Most of the papers will have been not *exercises in* how to write but *instances of* writing—writing about texts or problems that the student thinks are worth bothering about. It is not enough that teachers dish out what they consider tough stuff. Nor is it enough that students find their work engaging. What is required is that students become interested in material that is "too difficult" but not *too* difficult; it must demand that they figure out something to say on their own, without leaving them helpless.

3. Students will have encountered frequent critical responses from readers they respect. Some ecologist of mental resources should get working on the expense of spirit in a waste of shame represented by our annual accumulation of long, windy term papers simply deposited and graded, too often not even read. (I saw

5. There is even some empirical evidence for the effectiveness of most of them—though in such matters we seem never to discover decisive controlled experiments.

one, just last year, thirty pages returned with the sole comment: "A –. Some parts of this paper are much better than other parts.") The remaining practices follow from this one.

4. Course loads will have been small. Our various publics—the chairs and deans and presidents and boards and donors and taxpayers—must have been persuaded to support the most important and difficult of all educational tasks.

5. Mechanisms will have been found to ensure that students address *each other*. Some colleges have fortunate built-in traditions of discussion, traditions so powerful that it does not matter too much if courses do not get students to address each other. But most do not, and when that is so courses must artificially arrange for oral and written exchange, before and after each writing task.

6. Teachers of all subjects will have taken instruction in writing as part of their task. At every stage, students must expect their teachers, even in the hard sciences, to demand literate and interesting accounts. Every advanced course will have been thought of as in part a writing course. In short: "writing across the curriculum."

7. The literature they have read will have been broader than "literature." Though it will include novels, plays, poems, and short stories, it will range freely through all subjects that provide first-class writing. Distinctions between the "aesthetic" and other matters will be taken as problematic, not as established by departmental lines. The most immediately practical reason for this is of course that students need regular encounters with writing that resembles, at least remotely, what they are asked to write. But I hope that in what follows I can hint at considerably deeper motives. And in doing so I hope to show evidence for my third claim: that for sheer intellectual profit, the most "advanced" professor cannot afford to avoid regular assignments in that most noble of all educational tasks, teaching young people how to *compose*.

Since we can all name many subject matters that might satisfy my seven marks—some of them only remotely connected with "English" or "literature"—it will be well to think a bit about which subjects might be most strikingly qualified, assuming for the moment that we can find teachers to teach them. Quite obviously we do not, as a profession, agree on any list of such subjects. But each of us should be prepared to make a case in these terms for any subject, whether "literary" or not, that we ask our colleagues to require.

We can say this without repudiating the bromide one hears whenever, in curricular debate, someone proposes taking responsibility for narrowing students' choices: "There is no reason why a good course in *any* subject could not contribute to a liberal education, if taught properly." Of course. But obviously some subjects will prove less recalcitrant to liberal aims than others. To the degree that we have a choice of what we teach, we should try to devise courses around subjects that in themselves contribute to that special kind of hard thinking that is good writing.

After all this backing and filling, I want now to propose a possible sequence of rhetorical interests—perhaps it is better not to call them subject matters—that would make a defensible requirement for all college students (obviously the difficulty of the readings and the pace must vary depending on the students' previous preparation).[6]

We begin with one fundamental assumption about all of us, teachers and students alike: that we have an unlimited need, even

6. An increasing number of colleges have adopted the sensible practice of requiring a remedial course for those who are not ready for the basic "composition and literature." Such courses will merely compound the problems of the "split" we're talking about if those who staff them are isolated and exploited and even further down the academic ladder than those who teach the course that fills the writing requirement. My hunch is—though I have only scattered experience to prove it— that such courses can be at least partially redeemed from tedium and futility by planning them on the same rhetorical lines that I shall apply here to the "higher" level. The sequence I describe has never been taught in precisely this form, and it has never been tried on beginning students (my colleagues at the University of Chicago have for some years taught sequences somewhat like it in the "PERL major"—politics, economics, rhetoric, law).

Originally we called the year-long course filling the "rhetoric" component of PERL "Philosophy of Discourse." When students complained that it was not philosophical enough, we changed the name to "Practical Discourse." Now some of them complain that it is not *practical* enough. The sequence I offer here borrows not only from "Practical Discourse" but from (1) "Reading and Writing on Human Values," a freshman humanities course that Haverford College initiated in 1950, just before hiring me to direct it; (2) "Freshman Humanities" as we developed it at Earlham College; (3) "Humanities II" as developed in several versions in the University of Chicago's great "Hutchins College" of the 1940s; and (4) various "Humanities Common Core" versions developed as heirs to "Humanities II" from the mid-sixties to the present, especially a version with an unusually strong emphasis on composition, taught by a staff for three years now under the direction of Joseph Williams. Perhaps this is the place to say that the staff meetings for these courses have made the most important contribution to what little education I've managed to obtain.

when we don't know it, to improve our capacity *to shape reality with words*. The language we inherit, the language we all speak (in a sense "naturally," though it is obviously a cultural invention), is not on the whole adequate for tasks of reshaping and remaking reality; our unreflective speech serves best for repeating or reflecting realities already made by whatever has happened before the moment of speech. Spontaneous, unplanned speech is indeed a marvelous inheritance, one that works daily miracles. But it is a much more limited resource than we realize until we have discovered what can be made only with that secondary kind of language, the kind that is planned in advance.

What we do when we reflect for long on our speech before it is uttered—in most effective writing and public speaking—is to overcome or reshape the limiting realities imposed on us by our past. Put another way: we all encounter daily, in and out of formal schooling, innumerable efforts to "remake us," to reshape our responses and our worlds, usually to the advantage of the shaper and often to the disadvantage of the shaped. A college education should be, at a minimum, a period of learning both how to defend oneself against destructive shapings and how to remake oneself and one's circumstances through the mastery of what William Coles calls "premeditated discourse."

The sequence is thus organized around the question, What kinds of reality can be made only—or made best—with planned, artful speech? The alternative questions, central to many of the best composition courses employing rhetorical concepts, run more like this: What kinds of persuasion can be effected with words? How can we better get our way in the world by improving our mastery of discourse? My question obviously overlaps these at many points, but the shift to "making new realities with our discourse" is just unconventional enough to lead everyone, including the teacher, into new thinking.

For some the very notion of making realities with words will be a surprise: "What is *real* is one thing, what is *said* is another." "Actions are real, and they speak louder than words." "Less talk and more action." "Deeds not words" (a feminist slogan at the turn of the century). By questioning the assumed dichotomy between rhetoric and reality we open a whole range of questions that it either dismisses or settles by fiat: What is the difference between faking a reality and making one? Are "self-fulfilling prophecies" always a bad thing? What kinds of reality are in fact malleable, changeable, "remakable" with skillful discourse and what kinds, if any, are fixed? To what degree have "I" been made out of the words I have "consumed"? Am "I" a single voice or a collection of inherited voices? If I listen to new voices, if I take them in, what happens to the previous "me"? And how do I decide which voices shall be allowed to "remake" me?

But in the classroom I do not begin with such threatening questions. They spring from discussion of four kinds of making that are achieved, or botched, with discourse. There is nothing magical or original about my four kinds. They are implicit in every serious treatise on rhetoric: With our discourse we can (1) make or remake our characters and commitments in the *present;* (2) we make and remake (as "revisionists") our *past;* (3) we help to make our *future;* and (4) we sometimes hope to shape accurate reports on what is "neither past nor passing nor to come," since all of us "at one time or another"—note the phrase—attempt a "rhetoric of the timeless."

Remaking the Present

Image/Self/Ethos/Character   A good place to begin is with the making and remaking of people, "real" and imaginary. Students all have a small ready-made vocabulary for such makings: they see themselves *as* selves, personalities, characters, persons, individuals. They talk about images and reputations. Some of them have run across more sophisticated versions: mask, persona, ethos, identity. They also come with a rich collection of opinions about who the "real" person is, how it is made or found, in contrast with what is phony or faked, insincere, hypocritical. So they all, even the least literate, have a stake in notions of what sorts of self-presentation are legitimate, and they are thus ready to discuss how a given text creates an ethos of the speaker or implied author.

One can begin with any text so long as it *appears* fairly easy. But an especially good beginning, I've found, is any piece of current political rhetoric by someone skillful in making the right ethos for the occasion. In 1980, just after the Democratic National Convention, an obvious choice was Senator Kennedy's "farewell" speech to the convention. The speech is full of overt appeals to Kennedy's character, as against the unmentioned doubts about his past. Since most of my students were aware that the convention had been in part played out against the question whether the man of Chappaquiddick was adequate to the presidency, it seemed natural to them to talk explicitly about his various efforts to "remake" himself before our eyes. The better students saw much of the evidence for remaking even on first reading, but we were all surprised at just how many references we found to the *kind of man speaking*.

Obviously that particular speech will never work quite so well again; next time I must find something else that is topical—an editorial from the student newspaper, a copy of a student's letter of application, an acceptance speech by the latest and best-known Nobel Prize winner. The important thing is to get them quickly into seeing that every speaker "makes" a self with every word uttered; that even the most "sincere" statement implies a self that is at best a radical selection from many possible roles; and that we are thus in some degree free to choose which of our "selves" to present. Whether we judge what we do as dishonest or not, no one in fact "comes on" in exactly the same way with parents, roommates, teachers, classmates, lovers, and IRS inspectors. The next step is to realize that we do not present the same ethos at different periods in our lives; the collection of "selves" from which we draw in addressing lovers and parents and shoe clerks itself changes from decade to decade, and the question then arises: To what degree can we choose the direction of change? And what are the differences between growth and decay? By now the class is beginning to see ways in which "the self" is plastic, whether we want it to be or not.[7]

Ethos is thus a good place to begin, partly because students find the subject, if treated with some degree of aggression, totally new; they have not, in general, been taught to see how they reveal themselves—their selves—with every word they speak. Yet they already "know" a good deal about it. And they have an intuitive sense of their need for better control over their many selves. They are aware, for example, that they are in danger of betraying ignorance when they commit one or another of the innumerable errors that make "English" such a horrendous subject; no matter how many errors they clean out, their teachers have always been able to prove them clods, ignorant of further unsuspected rules.

7. Because of the recent history of the word "plastic" as a noun, it may give some difficulty at first. Students can find out a lot about how words work by looking up this one and its cousins—learning, for example, that God was once thought of as the great "plasmator."

They thus are already aware that they can choose a "cleaner ethos" just by consulting a dictionary. But they are less often aware that, along with clean or dirty surfaces, they are also creating selves that are timid or courageous, pedantic, pretentious, hostile, friendly, hectoring, wheedling, seductive, tough, sweet, or stuffy.[8] It seems new to them to discover how every author, regardless of subject or purpose, deliberately or accidentally creates an ethos that is always an inescapable part of what is communicated.

I move next to works in which the creation of character is even more explicitly central than in Kennedy's speech: Socrates building his total character as a lifetime enterprise in *The Apology;* Fra Lippo Lippi and Mr. Sludge, the medium, manipulating their victims in Browning's poems; Jane Austen creating admirable and ridiculous and contemptible characters in *Persuasion,* the author "betraying" Mr. Elliot with the subtlest of clues, establishing her hierarchy of strong and weak, tender and mean, witty and dull, wise and stupid (even the title makes a nice rhetorical point of reference for a course of this kind: persuasion to *what?*); Franklin in his *Autobiography* and Poor Richard self-consciously working out roles that can easily be shown to differ from other realities in his life; Prufrock giving himself away and simultaneously revealing an implied Eliot; Dostoevski's underground man shilly-shallying and exposing himself with every self-correction.

Perhaps it is by now obvious that in dealing with such matters it is impossible to distinguish what one does as a teacher of writing and as a teacher of literature. The best instruction in how to "read out" the various characters from such works, including the character of the implied authors, will be the best instruction in how to develop a powerful variety of voices in our own writing. I do not see how any professor of "literature" can be satisfied at any level, but especially in the early years of college, with instruction that leaves the students passively observing techniques and effects in what they read without practicing those techniques and seeking effects of their own. One reason so many potential majors in "English" are bothered by the question, "But what will I *do* with it?" is that their instruction has been passive in precisely

8. Those who know the history of modern efforts to get "voice" properly emphasized in composition teaching will recognize that I here quote the title of Walker Gibson's *Tough, Sweet, and Stuffy: An Essay on Modern American Prose Styles* (Bloomington: Indiana University Press, 1966).

this sense. No student who had actually *done* something with it, *as the education was going on,* could be bothered by that question.

For this reason—and not just because we are talking about a writing course—students should be expected, from the very beginning, to try out various voices and to receive criticism about whether they have hit the right tone for a specified task. It is not that they are asked to write *about* themselves; they write *with* one or another of their various selves, after thinking about how it relates to a given audience and a specified purpose.

There may be some papers devoted to analyzing the voices in the literature read, and others might be on any traditional topic. But in every paper the students should be expected to think about who they are trying to be, or seem to be, as they address a specific audience, that audience explicitly described in a separate note to the reader. If they are trying to be "a bright college student impressing a learned professor," they must think about how one does that, and about the pitfalls that might betray their act. If they are trying to write just naturally, "like myself" (and some will at the beginning insist that *that* is the only honest way to write), they should learn to expect criticism from their fellow students about what that self seems to be once it is written down.

Obviously for such a course the teacher must not be the only reader. Students must read each other's papers and engage in controversy about who is addressing whom. I find that things work best when I manage to meet students at least once every other week in small group tutorials of four to six students. They are asked to make enough copies of their short papers so that each can read all the papers before tutorials begin, and our hour (or longer: students often ask to have the period continue) is spent discovering whether understanding has occurred or why it has not. Such tutorials are not generally peaceful. Students learn, painfully, that their colleagues find them bullying, pedantic, ignorant, silly, dull, or sycophantic (though that's not the term they use). Their feelings get hurt. They develop friends and enemies. They recover. They go away and try again.[9]

9. I first ran into the use of such tutorials at Haverford in 1950 and then wrote, with Ralph Sargent, an account of why they were for me a revelation: "Reading and Writing on Human Values," *Journal of General Education* 5 (1951): 245–53. I then took the idea to Earlham, and later to Chicago, where we obtained a Danforth Foundation grant to experiment further with it. Unlike most of the experimental programs I have had anything to do with, this one seems to endure,

And most students quickly learn the fun of trying out voices they have never before dared to be. Whatever else can be said about starting a LITCOMP course in this manner, it is the best way I know to get students to enjoy their writing and to care about succeeding with it. The chief danger, in fact, comes to be a kind of overenthusiasm. Some students soon feel they have been liberated to lie to the world at will: "If I can mimic *anybody,* maybe there are no limits." And soon one finds letters to the campus newspaper written in very strange voices indeed—ironic, deceptive, a bit out of control, attempting effects that are not yet quite manageable. Thus the few students who dig in their heels and refuse to be anything but "themselves" are important as a source of questioning about the ethical limits of manipulating ethos.

The borderline between honest and dishonest creation of ethos has always been problematic, and it always will be. When students begin, they think they know where to draw the line: one should be *sincere*. When they discover that every piece of writing in a sense makes a "character" who is almost always an improvement over the spontaneous, undoctored person who wrote it, they suddenly fear hypocrisy. In place of the usual anxieties felt by freshman writers—"the teacher will find errors," "I will fail," "I have nothing to say"—we tend to find students fearing their newfound glibness. The black student who is freed to write his argument in street language, addressing a hostile gang, may suddenly become afraid about what we are letting loose: Can *that* kind of talk have anything to do with college education or "good English"? Some of the more perceptive students will begin to worry about the whole subject of rhetoric (whether the word has occurred in class or not), just as Socrates worried about the Sophists. It occurs to them that the more skillful we become in inventing voices not genuinely our own, the more dangerous we are. Some of our best discussions and papers come as students explore the ways their present "selves" have been constituted by the roles they have "tried on" in the past, and as they ask where hypocrisy leaves off and honest growth begins. They are not, they realize, the fixed core of "real me" that much of our thinking about language suggests. "Who am I *really?*" is never a simple question with a single

---

in various forms and degrees of precariousness, at all three places. From one point of view it is expensive in time and energy; but I am convinced that if one could ever do a genuine cost-benefit analysis, it would turn out to be cheap.

answer. Some students will, early in the course, ask whether they can write short stories or poems deliberately creating alien characters, while in a subtler sense discovering new characters for themselves. The answer is yes, yes, yes—so long as you are willing to reflect with your fellow students on what you have created.

By the end of such a unit, the students have discovered in their reading some scores of characters made with words—both the explicitly created characters and the implied authors of literary works and of their classmates' papers. And they have created six or eight voices of their own, some of them deliberately imitated from those in our readings.

Audiences/Readers   Just as every human utterance implies the kind of self who would utter it, so it implies an addressee who can understand it. Every stroke examined in studying ethos can be turned around and viewed as a stroke that creates an audience, the kind of audience capable of dealing with the issues or emotions at hand. Kennedy reconstituted, at least for a few moments, an audience of committed "New Deal liberals" who longed for a leader like him. I thus find it useful to review, as we begin the second unit, all the texts of the first unit, underlining the way our pursuit of ethos on the first run may have obscured other "makings."

In dealing with audience making, students see even more clearly than in talking of ethos just how impoverished is the view of rhetoric as persuasion to propositions. The point is perhaps best made by beginning with works that are clearly epideictic like Lincoln's "Gettysburg Address" or Pericles' "Funeral Oration," but advertising blandishments also work well. Speakers and writers who set out to reaffirm or implant "values" or "commitments" inevitably attempt to make or remake communities as they do so. The outcome of such rhetoric is never reducible to a specific list of propositions or values. An audience moves, when such rhetoric is successful, to embrace a new character for itself, one that can join that of the speaker.

But of course the effect is not confined to explicitly epideictic rhetoric like Lincoln's or Pericles'. Just as a speaker's ethos can be extracted, in analysis, from every human statement, so can an implied audience be extracted from anything we say. In this respect the "purest" poetry is as didactic as a political pamphlet:

"Please become the kind of person who can read me," it cries, even when what is audible seems to be only private whisperings.

After playing for a week or two with audience makings, spontaneous and doctored, "literary," didactic and conversational, students will begin to speculate about the degree to which such makings endure as permanent effects in them—in what they will think of still as the "real" world. All of us take on roles as readers and listeners, just as we do when we speak or write. Do we afterward drop those roles casually, indifferently, and return to face our "real selves"? Or do we become a kind of accumulation of the roles we have allowed ourselves to play? How do we deal with those texts that ask us to play roles we refuse? Of the roles we have learned in the past, which ones should be allowed into dialogue with whatever new demands we meet? Just how plastic *are* we? How plastic should we *allow* ourselves to be?

No teacher of "literature" will find such questions unworthy of full attention; no "composition" teacher will find such questions unconnected with learning how to write. Students who look seriously at the roles they are asked to play will of course be looking very closely at how the demands are made by the text: they will be learning how to read and simultaneously building their own repertory of rhetorical resources. But of course that repertory should again be made active by regular writing assignments that go beyond the usual textual analysis. Instead of routine requests to figure out what the text has said, teachers of LITCOMP will invent assignments that require that figuring out while leading students to remake audiences for themselves.

At least part of the time they should be asked to invent their own situations: "Imagine that you face hostile readers whom you must turn around if you are to win their support for some cause you care about. Think hard about why they are hostile—about their own values and about why you seem to represent the enemy. Then construct a speech or pamphlet designed to reconstitute them as in fact friendly (to their great surprise) to your cause." One student last year addressed his classmates with a moving appeal against their view of him as a conceited slob; another addressed a hostile student senate determined to impeach him as president. It is easy to find both literary examples (Mark Antony's speech over Caesar's body) and current political examples. As I write, in December 1981, I would probably use one of Reagan's recent speeches—to hostile labor leaders, or to the convention of suspicious and threatened mayors.

It is not hard for students to find either in their personal lives, in what they can "get up" quickly about the world around them, in literature, or in their imaginations, "circumstances" to be re-made. They are required to make clear in a note at the beginning "who the author is trying to be," "who the readers or listeners are, and in what respect they are opposed," and "who they are intended to become by the end of the piece." Some of the best papers come from students who choose to write letters to people they know—persuading their parents to allow them a year abroad, asking a wealthy aunt for a loan or gift, pleading with a boyfriend for one more chance. It is true that such "personal" assignments, given without proper intellectual preparation, can become sentimental ways of escaping education. But when students are required to put in writing a brief account of what the rhetorical problem is, and when they are expected later to defend to fellow students the means they have adopted, there is no problem either about intense engagement or about intellectual substance.

Toward the end of any section on audience constitution it is important to engage in some work that is at the outer reaches of a given class's abilities. My students at Chicago find Burke's *Reflections on the Revolution* and *The Education of Henry Adams* almost too tough to endure at first, which means that they are just about right by the end.

It would not worry me at all that colleagues might complain about my neglecting "substance" in such work. In the first place, at each step we would necessarily be encountering what they mean by substance; you can't talk about how to remake an audience without talking about the *substantive* arguments that a given audience can be expected to hear and respond to. In the second place, the making of a persuasive speaking voice and the reshaping of audiences is itself, in this view, as substantive as syllogisms. If what Lincoln did at Gettysburg in creating a noble leader of a high-minded, united, and committed people was not, in that situation, a matter of substance, it is hard to think what would have been. And on the other hand, the substance of any great novel or poem is—that is, can be viewed as—the reshaping of characters.

But it is important that the course, whether confined to one year as I would prefer, or extended to two full years, include makings that to many seem more substantive than ethos and audience. Students will of course have discovered, all along, that every speaker makes many other "things," other realities, in every successful utterance, regardless of the ostensible writing task. I doubt that it matters very much which of the following "makings" are chosen. What is essential is to see that writing well is not a matter of cleaning up something like "style" or "mere rhetoric" but deals with *changing what is real.*

Making the Past in Story: Fiction, Journalism, History

Every student comes to college with an intuitive sense that there is somehow a difference between a made-up story and a report on what "actually happened." The imagination is free, while the reporter or historian should be bound to some conception of "the facts." It seems as natural as breathing to ask of a storyteller, "Was he lying or telling the truth?"

Some current theorists—perhaps the best know is Hayden White—have made a good deal out of questioning this distinction, reminding us that every historical account is an invented story, a "fiction," and that all we have as the history of our past is a collection of such stories: "history" is no more than our accumulated fictive effort.[10] On another front, many a popular storyteller has been blurring the intuitive distinction between truth and fiction.[11]

Though I think it important not to push such extreme positions onto students at any point, it is equally important to lead them to see that the intuitive distinction, though perhaps finally in some sense justified, raises more problems than it solves. Taken at face value, it solidifies the popular distinction between what is real, established, fixed, like "nature," and what is unreal, "mere rhetoric," "merely made up," "a product of the imagination." The distinction is false not because there is no difference between writing *Pride and Prejudice* and writing Tocqueville's *L'Ancien Régime,* but because the lines are usually drawn in the wrong

10. See Hayden White's *Metahistory: The Historical Imagination in Nineteenth-Century Europe* (Baltimore: Johns Hopkins University Press, 1973) and his "The Value of Narrativity in the Representation of Reality," *Critical Inquiry* 7 (1980): 5–27.

11. We may deplore the blurring, especially when it exploits and increases the suffering of real people, as I think Norman Mailer does in *The Executioner's Song.* But it is not new (think of Defoe) and it is not likely to go away.

places in the wrong way. Every storyteller makes realities, and every storyteller uses imagination and emotion. Every storyteller creates patterns of causation. There is nothing more solidly real in the picture of the past created by Tocqueville than in the fictional world created by Jane Austen, if by real we mean something that has power to affect who we are and what we do. But the realities are surely somehow different, and it is an important part of every writer's education to have thought about the differences and to have practiced the arts of making different portraits of what happened or what might have happened.

A good path into the jungle of problems encountered in making stories is simple reporting. I begin by trying to invent some new version of that old exercise used in elementary psychology texts: stage some dramatic event, as shockingly and yet as realistically as possible, and have the students write an account of it from memory. Have them compare their conflicting accounts, and they will learn, once and for all, that even "true stories" are in some sense invented. The exercise may seem hackneyed to us, and students today may have experienced it in other college courses or in high school; that's why one must be inventive, never repeating a given staged event, and never allowing the students to jump to the misleading conclusion that all accounts are equally valid.

I find it useful in our discussion to move, with seeming confidence, to a moment when I can say, "Now let's compare what you *thought* happened—all these conflicting accounts—with what *really* happened." I then give them the "true version"—the episode as I planned it—and wait for the inevitable moment when someone realizes that even the account by the stage manager is not absolutely privileged, not acceptable as flatly true without critical consideration of purposes, biases, limitations.

Without spending more than two days on this exercise (one that has included a writing assignment, of course), I move quickly to something from the "real world," a public event as reported by journals with different biases—the "same event" as reported by the *Christian Science Monitor, Time Magazine,* the *Wall Street Journal,* and my hometown paper. We may think such an exhibit of pandemic unreliability is already self-evident to our students. Not so. Some of them do think of themselves as cynical about the reliability of the news. But they will all usually accept whatever single account they have read. And when they do become "critical" they are likely to conclude that, because the accounts are "all biased," all of them are equally worthless. What is hard is to see that a collection of the most serious and responsible accounts of any event is "all we have," but that at the same time there are ways of discovering that some accounts are better than others. It is easy to teach cynicism about journalism—and about history. It is harder to develop students' arts of discrimination and to lead them to try for a responsible kind of making.

These first two brief exercises are preliminary to a large section built around some major event that has attracted a fair number of serious writers. Our staffs often use the French Revolution, as imagined by Michelet, Edmund Burke, Tocqueville, perhaps Carlyle or Dickens, and some more recent historians. But any event that can be labeled as "something everyone agrees happened" will do: a world war, any other revolution, any other major war, the Depression, "Watergate," "the Holocaust."

The main writing assignments throughout the discussion of "story" again should not be analyses of other stories. Students should themselves face the task of making stories that make reality. "Write a convincing account of what happened." I have had fine papers on topics ranging from family history ("How and Why My Grandparents Came to America") to "What Really Happened at the First Gate the Day the Bastille Fell?" and "Why Did Nixon Resign?" Experienced composition teachers will recognize that such topics resemble in some respects the "Research Paper" unit in older composition texts. They require the student to master the research and writing techniques that were pursued in those exercises, but they do it in a context that unites the class in a common endeavor: thinking about how we make and remake the past, and criticizing other people's makings. Of course some students choose to attempt fictional narration as their special task.

Making the Future: Constitutions, Laws, Deliberations, Polemic

Just as an emphasis on making and remaking the past can revitalize the traditional drill on "narrative," so an emphasis on making the future brings life to assignments in "argument." Every student, however badly prepared, has experienced debates that have changed the future—if only disputes in family or gang. Every student has taken part in making constitutions—if only disputes

about which rules will apply in a given game. And by the time
we come to this subject, all students have participated in establishing whatever conventions of discussion operate, however tacitly, in the class. They are thus ready for some kind of unit on
"The Making of Constitutions," or (somewhat less ambitiously)
"Legal Rhetoric—'Real' and 'Literary.' "

Again one can start as simply as the experience of the students
dictates. The class can watch reality change right before their
eyes if they are asked to debate about what should be read next
(I would not want to do this more than once a term, and in the
right spot; in the name of freedom it was badly overdone in the
late sixties); or about whether to adopt rules controlling who
speaks when; or even, if things get desperate, about whether to
have a party, and what kind. What is important is to work up
quickly from the obvious to the toughest intellectual challenge
they can hope to meet.

We have found sufficiently tough going—and what feels like
success—with various units on "The Making of Constitutions,"
working up through simpler tasks to a comparison of the American
Constitution with the "ideal" constitution constructed at about
the same time by Rousseau. Some of them think, of course, that
they already know our Constitution, but none of them has ever
looked at it with real care. Every word in that strange and wonderful piece of committee work has changed the world in some
respect or other, while the much more obviously perfected and
inspiring constitutions from the philosophers have been forgotten
except by historians.

To study why the one piece of rhetoric differs so much in its
effects from the others, one must know some of the choices the
Constitutional Convention faced. Fortunately, we have a rich
record about its making and remaking, most notably Madison's
Notes on the Constitutional Convention, *The Federalist Papers,*
and the Marshall decision (*Marbury* vs. *Madison*) on the role of
the Supreme Court. And we have reminders almost every week
of the role those documents still play in shaping present reality.

Students who have once seen how the Constitution was carved
out of the diverse and conflicting interests and ideals of the founding fathers are not likely to fall into current simplifications about
rhetoric: that it is somehow less real that "action"; that learning
to "do" it is learning to put the icing on the cake; that the goal
of writing is only to be simple and clear (no one has ever worked

harder to be productively and deliberately ambiguous than did the founders); or that learning to write is something separable from getting a genuine education. Indeed, the founding fathers' act of reconstituting their world and ours, of remaking the future by reconstituting and relocating speakers and audiences and situations in the present and reshaping the past, can be viewed as a kind of paradigm of the powers of self-conscious "rhetoricians" transforming the world by providing guarantees that future rhetorical exchange will be both possible and productive.[12]

Space will not allow me to pursue in detail other kinds of making that might well be adopted by particular staffs. An obvious possibility would be "The Making of Cultures," borrowing from cultural anthropologists and social historians but also looking at "literary" works as both reflections of and shapers of cultural codes or "worlds." Perhaps the richest current literature about reality making in rhetoric is that of anthropologists who study how peoples constitute each other in symbolic exchange. Or one might attempt a category that does not appear in traditional rhetorical theories, what we might call "Making for All Time: Philosophy, Religion, Science." If things have gone as they should, students will have encountered from the beginning many questions about how attempts to state permanent truths relate to the realities they have been making in rhetoric. If new realities can be made by choosing *these* words rather than *those* words, what is reality *really?* If even the efforts of scientists to fix reality in words turn out to shift from decade to decade, if every philosophical or religious document yields different meanings to different interpreters or different cultures, is there nothing that endures?

I think I would not attempt this unit unless I were sure we had time enough to avoid the two obvious pitfalls: my imposing *my* notion of enduring truths, and their electing a premature and uninformed relativism. And there is another problem with "attempting permanence." Though it is easy to think of texts, including great "literary" works, for reading assignments, it's a bit harder to think of the *active* writing assignments that have come easily in the earlier units I have described. The proper activity

12. I owe most of what I know and feel about the usefulness of these constitutional materials to staff meetings with my colleague David Smigelskis, who is completing a book that will "reconstitute," among other things, our definitions of rhetoric.

for this section is "thinking about what's true," and students need a long period of grappling with first-class texts before they can do that without floundering. Whether I would include it in my sequence would thus depend, I think, on whether I were given two years or one. What I would really like to see some bold college attempt is to develop a *three*-year LITCOMP sequence, the third-year course (to be taken in the final year of college) being a serious encounter with the problems suggested by the notion of "timeless rhetoric." Given such a year, I would of course include in my readings a fair number of texts *about* education and about how different theories of knowledge and of rhetoric interrelate. In short, given world enough and time, I would have every college graduate experienced in writing about how human beings have thought about how human beings think.

My sequence is clearly a course (or courses) in rhetoric, yet I have so far mentioned no text *about* rhetoric. How much explicit reading of rhetorical theory and analysis the students should read— how much they should read *about* how we think about thinking— must depend on who they are and on the interests and capacities of particular staffs.

In our recent experience, my colleagues and I have been reluctant to introduce even the greatest of "rhetorics," Aristotle's, until fairly late; we fear the tendency of students to use any systematic text as a crutch, and our fear seems to be justified by what we know of the history of rhetoric and rhetorics. At the same time, we know that students are shortchanged if they are thrown into the vast amorphous domains of human symbolic exchange without assistance from those who have traveled before them. I would thus want to ensure some sort of systematic assistance from theoretical texts or surveys of the arts: if not rhetoric, then "philosophy of science" or "speech-act theory," broadened to "philosophy of discourse that claims to be cognitive," or the best work of cultural anthropologists who have thought about how cultures are constituted in discourse. I can imagine a fine section of a course reading Clifford Geertz, Marshall Sahlins, Nancy Munn, John Comaroff, and Michael Silverstein, to name only those I happen to know, and then asking the students to *do* some cultural anthropology on their own cultures. Indeed, every field I know anything about, including by now even law, has begun to produce what can be called metarhetorics of the disciplines, inquiring into what can be known about our ways of knowing, or what can be said about our ways of saying. What is most important is that students be asked not just to study the texts but to *do* something *like* the text, to *practice* the rhetoric the texts exhibit, and then to reflect, as those named have done, on that practice.

It should be clear by now why no writing course of this kind can be turned over to a "composition" staff. Designing and teaching it will require the joint efforts of young and old, experienced and inexperienced, specialists in many different fields, those who are most learned and those who have been lassoed off the streets. In such a course, everyone will have something to teach and something to learn.

To say as much suggests why it is that serious professors of "literature" cannot afford to leave such courses to the peons. Students in such courses will learn to love what they are doing, and they will want to do more of it. If they have come to enjoy wrestling with ideas, both in speaking and in writing, and if they see that advanced "literature" professors have nothing to do with the course where they have learned to care about such matters, they will rightly choose to major in other fields. But if those professors who know the world's best "literature," those who are committed to the great "literary" classics, become engaged in such courses, they will have no trouble convincing their colleagues and their students that the richest, the most serious, the most important makings of selves, communities, nations, and cultures have been achieved, after all, by the composers of great literary works, an astonishing number of which are what I've been calling "literature." Any professor of "literature" working with such a staff will have no shame in insisting that large blocks of time be taken up with great classics of English and American "literature," because he or she will know, and be able to show, that such classics supply kinds and intensities of making that no other form of literature can provide. Those of us who are professors of "literature" as well as of rhetoric never experience a hard-and-fast divorce between what we do when we read or write about Aristotle and about Shakespeare. Though we do tend to ask and answer different questions about different kinds of texts, we also play tricks on ourselves and our texts by reversing what seems the "natural" order of questions, turning upon our favorite thinkers questions about their aesthetic value, or upon our favorite poets questions about their truthfulness or moral worth or capacity to build cultures.

Anyone who has ever taken part in planning a required course knows the vast distance between idea and practice. If it were easy to install and staff courses of the ambitious kind I have suggested here, we would have more of them. But it is painfully obvious that our problems run deeper than my superficial account suggests, and that the forces working against any reintegration of the kind I've called LITCOMP are immense. My effort to dream up one possible course is designed to work against only one of those forces—our own temptation to be self-protective and inert. But I know that even if we all changed our ways—those of us who are "here" in a book of this kind—we would be combating historical and economic forces that nobody fully understands and that may very well not be reversible.

But we cannot know unless we try, and we cannot try without thinking, longer and harder than we have ever done, about where we are and how we got here and how we might remake ourselves and our circumstances—in the very spirit of the course sequence I have described. We are presumably the best-trained rhetoricians in the country. Unless that training has been only in how to write passable "literary criticism," we ought to be able, working together, to discover ways of remaking our profession.

5   Discerning Motives in Language Use
David Bleich

It is widely held in the language and literature profession that, while literature and composition are both central subjects in the domain of "English," they are essentially separate. There has been a "standard" way of relating them to one another—by having students write "compositions" about "literature"—but this rarely leads anyone to believe that the two subjects are intrinsically or conceptually related. The separation is underscored by the circumstance that, as numbers of English "majors" decline, students from other, "preprofessional" disciplines are increasingly required to take courses that "teach them how to write"; such students have no real reason to write about literature, but they need to learn to write in a wider sense. It is taken for granted that "at least" a certain level of technical proficiency is teachable and that, even if it is not, a great effort in "practicing" writing will increase a person's technical proficiency, which is all students (and other departments) want anyway. From this circumstance comes the irritating thought that teachers of composition are performing a "service" for the rest of the university. What has happened is that English teachers have collaborated in the public devaluation of their subject.

There is no quick way to overturn this burdensome syndrome of beliefs and practices. It is not simply a professional attitude that must be changed; it is presuppositions about what language is, and thus how literature is related to language, how writing is related to it, and how teaching is related to literature and writing. To approach these issues in their practical dimensions, I will present, with examples, a relatively simple proceeding that can be undertaken in the classroom or by any other group of two or more people either speaking to one another or writing for one another's interest: the discernment of motives in language use. Of course, a detailed justification for this is necessary, but merely presenting the proceeding will suggest ways the conception of language must be changed to create a sense of unity in the study of literature and of writing. The goal is to see language as inter-subjective rather than objective.

A motive is not radically different from an intention, but an *intention* is conceived in connection with *intentionality*. Intentionality can be described as a "long-term" motive, or an abiding motive, or a kind of underlying orientation of one's language habits in effect in an individual's particular developmental phase. Thus an intention is the subjective sense of why one is using language at the moment, and an intentionality is a collection of options for making decisions about using language, governed by the phase-specific needs of each person. (I am using the concept of the developmental phase as outlined by Erikson in his discussion of life-cycle phases in *Childhood and Society*.) To discern motives in language use, one must be ready to recognize both intention and intentionality.

It is impossible to discern motives by perusing a single text or a single language act. Although it is usually a simple matter to make *sense* of a single text, speech, or item of conversation, it requires *negotiation* between the sense maker and the speaker or writer to discern motives for the language act. This discernment is not unlike the familiar practice of interpretation, except that it can come *only through* negotiation. The final authority for the agreement on both intention and intentionality is thus intersubjective. Even before negotiation, however, any single text must be viewed in juxtaposition with another text by the same author or with some *con*text other than the text itself yet related to it. Discerning the motives of a language act presupposes that that act is in some syntactical circumstance that first permits the motives proposed to be authorized by subsequent negotiation.

A text or language act is always in some syntactical circumstance, in that it can be understood only in relation to something else; there are an indefinite number of predicates for any text or "subject." The sense maker may either choose the syntactical circumstance of interest or negotiate a common one with the author or speaker, but motives cannot be discerned unless such a circumstance is established. The text or language act has no functional meaning until its syntactical role is stipulated. Functional meaning is the same as intention or intentionality in that it refers to the pragmatic part that language act plays within the context of its presentation. Therefore interpreting a text is the same as discerning motives associated with it; however, discerning motives requires intersubjective negotiation, while ordinary interpretation is private. Discerning motives is a proceeding that depends on a view of language that yields a unified conception of "literature" and "composition" inquiries, while ordinary interpretation is confined to the reading of literature and is regularly distinguished from things like technical proficiency, the composing process, and "writing well."

In demonstrating this proceeding I will give two instances of "negotiated" meaning in a "composition" and a third instance in which a syntactical circumstance makes it possible to propose motives as meanings and unifies the study of literature and composition.

Question: Think back to the first time in your life that a verbal or language event scared you. Name the person speaking, describe the full circumstances, and discuss the extent to which a purely verbal event (someone saying something) is fearful. Describe your fearful feelings as fully as possible and explain the significance of this event today.

Answer: (given in thirty minutes' writing time) The first recall I have of someone saying something that frightened me was when I was four years old and my grandmother told me that if I swallowed my bubble gum all my insides would stick together. My imagination then told me that one of two horrible fates would overtake me, either, I would swell up and bust or I would die of starvation.

To this day I don't enjoy chewing gum and just the sight of someone else chewing it makes me queasy. During my first grade-school years, I, of course, told all my chums what chewing gum could do to them and one of them asked the teacher if it was true. A very concerned Mrs. W (third grade) drew me aside and told me that chewing or swallowing gum could not hurt you and would I please stop scaring the rest of the students.

To say the least this confused me and caused me to distrust and not speak to my grandmother for about four months, but the enlightenment from the teacher never did quite cure me of my fear or slight phobia of chewing gum.

This may not be considered by some people a very big deal, but consider how many children and adults chew gum and what it would be like to actually be made sick by it.

This essay was negotiated—discussed—in a class of twenty-five other freshmen and me. The main discussion point was Ms. S's claim that to this day she retains a "slight phobia" about gum chewing. The negotiative context was the goal of verifying or explaining both the claim and the person making the claim. In a sense Ms. S's integrity was also being tested, since the class did not quite believe one could remain phobic about gum chewing after an event such as Ms. S reported. Thus, in inquiring about Ms. S's motive, the question is whether she is genuinely sharing something or is less than sincere; or, what is her motive for presenting the "slight phobia," or, finally, what does "slight phobia" really mean, relative to Ms. S's intention, intentionality, and membership in this class?

The definitive question was asked by another student, who wanted to know Ms. S's actual relationship with her grandmother. Ms. S reported that grandmother, her mother's mother, had dominated her mother, who was divorced from her father a year later. The grandmother, in other words, was the authority figure in the family, and this accounts for the very strong effect she had on Ms. S. If we understand that the grandmother has remained the authority figure to this day, the abiding "slight"phobia about gum chewing is believable and, further, has a specific sense, or meaning, or scope. Without an inquiry such as took place in class, one cannot understand the "meaning" of Ms. S's "words," even though their sense is clear.

Ms. S's intention is to answer the question and report something authentic—though not too intimate—to the class. Her intentionality is to juxtapose to the class one of her historical sources of authority, to enter the peer group with something genuine about herself—the gum-chewing fear—yet to describe it in such a way as to help deauthorize the grandmother. This intentionality should be understood as characteristically adolescent. However, until the negotiation actually takes place neither the intention nor the intentionality can be understood; only when they are thus understood can one say that Ms. S's *language* has been understood. In this example the syntactical circumstance is the classroom purpose. Ms. S's essay is the subject, and its predicate is its negotiation in class; together there is a "sentence" whose meaning (intention and intentionality) or motives has been disclosed in the terms described above.

Here is a second instance of negotiated meaning, one in which I played a more central role in the negotiation with the student.

Question: Describe at least one feature of your instructor's language (spoken and/or written) that he/she might not know about and that you think he/she should be aware of. How does this feature contribute to your understanding of the instructor as a person, and why should he/she be made aware of it?

Answer: (given in thirty minutes' writing time) One of the things I have noticed about Mr. Bleich's language is his ability to cut down others. Whether he does this intentionally or just out of habit—I don't know. I *do* know that when someone arrives to class late—you know there will be some comment made as to their tardiness. Even in his writings there are some of the same feelings that you would get if he were cutting some one down. His writings reflect his argumentative and aggressive style. By cutting others down I think he can let these feelings out. By also cutting others down he can show he is in control. I mean—not many people would try to defend themselves in front of a whole classroom! Maybe—subconsciously his cutting down of others only builds up his ego? I have heard that if a person cuts others down a lot they do it because they themselves feel insecure—?

Cutting others down is just a part of your style, Mr. Bleich. I don't think you build your ego up by cutting them down. I also don't think you are insecure. I think this way because of the way you speak—your spoken language.

Another thing I find interesting is your use of profanity vs. the use of big words. It seems that by using profanity we (the class) will be able to identify with you (you think). Maybe by speaking this way you think you are more on our level and will be accepted more readily. At the same time you use big words. This shows your high education. I think of these 2 language features as opposite and wouldn't expect to find them together in the same essay. It just seems as if there is an incongruity.

I think that you should be aware that some people feel threatened when you cut them or others down. You don't even know the people and you cut them down—how do you expect them to trust you—no matter in what manner you cut down. I'm not sure why you use profanity and big words together. Probably just to remain on our level but at the same time gain respect from us.

In my freshman course I teach one discussion section, and five others are taught by my assistants. Ms. K (above) was in the section I teach, so that the original question was referring to the students' discussion section instructor; I am the principal instructor and lecturer.

In responding to this essay, I allowed immediately the proposition that "I cut others down" because, to one degree or another, I think this is true. I see it as more of a teasing than a "cut down," but I can understand Ms. K's view of my behavior, and I accept her sentiments and her observations. The feature of her essay that I thought pertained most to our relationship was her shift from third person to second person as she started her second paragraph, and this is what I wanted to negotiate with her in class, with all the other discussion section students present.

I asked the following question, both of Ms. K and of the class: "What would be the difference between what Ms. K actually wrote and the following formulation of the same transition (from first to second paragraphs): Although it is probably not true of Mr. Bleich, I have heard that people cut down others because they are themselves insecure and need to build up their egos." I tried to formulate, in other words, a similar sentiment without changing from third to second person. Ms. K said unhesitatingly that my sentence was not the same as her two sentences, and the discussion then proceeded to the two sentences in question. One student, Ms. N, took down minutes for this class, and here is her report of what then happened.

> Ms. A pointed out that there were more direct things in the first sentence. Ms. D said that maybe Ms. K was not real sure how she felt. Ms. R. added that maybe she wrote it and then thought Mr. Bleich might think something bad. Ms. K. agreed. Ms. S mentioned that she would write it and not worry about what Mr. Bleich thought.

This version corresponds closely enough to my recollection of how the class went for me to say it is a "true" account. We do not know, however, just what Ms. K had in mind by "something bad"; the term was introduced by someone else, and Ms. K only assented to it. In any event, Ms. K verified that her version was different from mine because hers shows that she *changed her orientation of thought while writing*. The point was verified again later in the discussion when the same Ms. R characterized her change as a "rush of feelings."

I do not think Ms. K's change of person came from a fear of my authority. Students are more likely to erase or cross out something they feel is offensive enough to jeopardize their standing with the teacher. At the same time, one sees from Ms. S's comment that she would not have recorded her thinking over the situation as Ms. K did, and she would not in any case have been guided by her "worry" about what I thought.

Ms. K was "sure" and yet not sure at the same time, as Ms. D suggested. What Ms. K's essay catches is the difference between thinking something and having to say it in its appropriate context. Her recognition of the difference, however, was uncensored—she just shifted to direct address and was able to develop a tone that could accommodate all her thoughts without making her feel she changed her opinions. She stands by the thoughts given in the first paragraph, but the change of person reflects that her sense of what she had written there *motivated* her to write a little differently in the following paragraphs. The class discussion brought out, with relative certainty, that this had happened.

There is less certainty about why it happened, but consider the following explanation. In the next essay Ms. K showed her own propensity toward sarcastic exaggeration as she recounted an incident where she spoke that way—though respectfully—to a fellow she was on a date with. In the essay following this, she recounted an incident in which her direct address to her father reassured her during a family incident. In facing her mother's anger and withdrawal, Ms. K took comfort from her father's observation that he and she were "alike." Ms. K's abiding motivation, therefore, or her intentionality, is related to a certain priority for directing language straight to the person she is thinking about. I believe she uses the presence of the other person to help regulate her strong thoughts. Her use of language depends in some important ways on the priority of speaking *to* someone over the option of speaking *about*.

To understand the "meaning" of any *single* language act, other acts are needed to create a context, and negotiation is necessary to verify and clarify the author's motivational bearing—and thus the intention and intentionality. Put another way, no single essay is self-explanatory, and people cannot understand its language in a consequential way just by reading the essay. Classroom negotiation discloses the context and reaches a provisional, collective decision, corroborated by the author, as to the meaning, purpose, and intentions of the language.

I will now suggest the general role of reading literature in this larger project of discerning motives in language use.

In the same sense that a second or third essay by the same author provides a "syntactical circumstance" for a first essay, essays written in response to literature create a coordinate body of work that permits us to propose motives for *both* bodies and for the individual's general use of language. Because of the nature of the case (in the following example), I will not discuss the public negotiation of proposed intentions but will confine myself to showing how the essays about literature create "another context" to be used in the study of both groups. I will then suggest why literature—and other symbolic forms of imaginary things—is especially suitable for this task.

Here are three samples from Mr. B's first group of essays—those dealing with himself and his experiences.

Question: (given in discussion section) In the time remaining, tell something about yourself that you consider important—something you would like others to know. Be as detailed as possible, and try to explain why you want people to know this particular thing.

Answer: I am from a small city in southern Indiana, and as one well knows, not much happens in a small farming community. The people are generally only concerned about their farms and have little interest in the rest of the world. I have all way tried to be just the opposite of the people in my town, so life would have a meaning and be interesting for me. I have traveled to Europe hoping to get a better perspective of the world and the way people think. When one is away from a people other than himself he has a different perspective about himself and others.

I believe that for one to enjoy and obtain satisfaction from the earth one must be able to go many places, the solid, liquid and gases of the earth. I started flying so I could see the earth from above, and add a whole new perspective to the earth and myself. I started traveling so I could see the solid of the earth, its beauty and history. I am starting scuba diving so I can enjoy the liquid part of the earth and yet add another perspective to my mind. With these three tools one can observe the earth where we live and better understand ourselves and others. I believe that since I was so opposite of the people in my town I became lonely, and in search for something to do I traveled to meet other people more like myself.

I am very impatient, I have found no reason, so I must have been born with this trait. I am also full of contradictions.

Question: Try to recall a comment or judgment about yourself, said to you, or to someone else in your presence, which remains important to you today. Discuss the extent to which you think the remark is true, and describe just how important the speaker of this remark was to you.

Answer: When I was 15 an amazing ability seemed to find me. During that winter I invented 13 objects and didn't know what to do with them. I started asking people how to patent inventions. I went to atterney after atterney all advising to see another. I finally found one that didn't know the exact steps but would work with me until the job was compleated. Time after time he said, "How do you do this?" "You must be a genious". These words expressed his interest in me and I was extremely impressed with his persistence in helping me. To this day the adventure and judgement of him of me made us very close friends. . . .

I also told an owner of a firm in a big city of my invention and he was quit impressed with my enginuity. My respect for him had allways been extremely high and our friendship very close. When someone with such power tells you that you came up with some very brilliant ideas it "makes your day." To this day both are very impressed with me and I am very impressed with them.

Question: From the way your instructor speaks, writes, and conducts himself in class, describe and justify what you think might be *behind* this public presentation. How close a "match" do you think there is between what you see on the outside and what you think is inside?

Answer: I believe that when Mr. M speaks he speaks with confidence. I base this upon the fact that one can almost watch the gears in his brain turn through his eyes. When he speaks it sounds like what he is saying has been thought about before and recorded for a later time, sort of a mechanical voice.

It is probably clear from these samples that we are not dealing with an ordinary student; the work implies things about its author that have only an indirect bearing on our interest in discerning motives in language use. However, the personal burdens borne by this student help us observe a feature of language use that appears in much subtler form in students of a more usual stripe.

Consider, therefore, with the foregoing provisos in mind, what I am calling the "machine" theme in these samples. In the first essay there is the "solid, liquid, and gas" description of the earth. The second essay cites the student's thirteen "inventions," none of which, by the way, he could describe either to me or to his discussion instructor, Mr. M. And in the third sample there is the perception of "gears" in Mr. M's brain and his "mechanical voice." There is a less clear interpersonal theme—his distinguishing himself from those of narrow interests in his hometown, his being recognized by powerful men in a big city, and his perception of premeditation in his instructor's speech. The question is what to make of these formulations, as well as the other interesting details of his writing—such as the misspellings, the propensity to repetition of words and phrases, and the vaguely melodramatic way of telling things. To engage these problems, consider the following sentences, taken from his essays written in response to certain short stories.

1. I can just picture this incident: two blacks, deep South, poor community, low intelligence. . . . If I were one of the neighbors I would have called the sanitarium and had those kids taken care off [sic]. [Response to barroom anecdote]

2. When you have something nice like Major de Spain's house you take care of it, keep it clean. Then when some scud comes barging in like he did, and doing damage, he should have been shot [sic] on his merry way. People like that shouldn't even be allowed near the house. The servant should have been armed to control such a person. ["Barn Burning"]

3. The old lady got on my nerves and I wished she would have a heart attack or stroke. . . . I think she got what she deserved at the end of the story. . . . I would not like being on a small, almost never traveled, unfamiliar road without a gun. If thickheaded Bailey would have carried a gun in the car he would have had no problem. ["A Good Man Is Hard to Find"]

4. I thought that if I were the watcher of the artist and after days (30 or so) of watching him, making sure he did not eat anything, and I then saw him eat something that he had hidden, I would make sure that that was the very last thing he even would have the chance to eat again. . . . I thought to myself how much I would have like to have been there while he was dying, it would have been very unpleasant for him . . . did the watcher get paid for his time [?] . . . I [sic] he did not get paid for the job I think I would have given him food and then shot him for payment. ["A Hunger Artist"]

5. The drunk in the bar [in "A Tree, a Rock, a Cloud"] reminded me of the old drunks in downtown [X]. One would just as soon run over them then look at them. They just seem like stumbling targets . . . for a car.

As with the previously cited instances, one essay will not tell whether a particular pattern or language feature is salient. For example, we may surmise a particular sense of the phrase "taken care off" (1) once we see that every other instance presents a prospective murder, with Mr. B the clearly implied murderer. In presenting these strong images, Mr. B is taking advantage of the customary license in discussing literature that permits one to "kill" literary figures in conversation. On the other hand, when such images appear in a series of five different essays, each written two or three weeks after the previous one, and with Mr. B's knowledge that they may be duplicated, read, and discussed by the whole class, this is a language act whose intentions and intentionality are not to be explained as an instance of some convention.

For obvious reasons this was not an occasion for "negotiation," so my reading of the connections between the experience essays and the literature essays should be taken as the attempt to demonstrate a principle and not an attempt to reach a conclusive understanding of Mr. B.

The theme of murder in the literature essays should be connected to the unparticularized relationships cited in the experience essays. Thus we should interpret the phrases "opposite of the people in my town" and "I became lonely" as an allusion to what must be a violent and radical separation of Mr. B from everyone else at home. It is likely that Mr. B's ordinary phrases refer to a painful ostracism that has an extreme "me versus them" quality, and the idea of "opposite" may very well embody the feelings of wanting to be loved versus wanting to kill when one is not loved. Accordingly, I would interpret the sentence "I am also full of contradictions" as an indirect allusion to this extreme struggle. In the second experience essay, the attorney and the urban businessman, both "powerful," have recognized Mr. B's own transcendental power. They have (to him) converted the underlying ostracism into unique distinction, where Mr. B is not merely loved, but admired, honored, and perhaps adored: "You must be a genious." Also, the phrase "I am very impressed with them" documents his precocious accession to adulthood and maturity rather than the admiration of a young man for older ones. Furthermore, in Mr. B's view, adults may be permitted to kill, while children are in the class of potential victims, along with blacks, nagging old ladies, drunks, and starving men. In describing his instructor, a real person he had to deal with from day to day, and who therefore could not be vaguely or unspecifically identified, he is more circumspect and confines himself to noting that Mr. M speaks with much premeditation. If we had not read any of Mr. B's other essays, in fact, there would be practically nothing unusual about his perception of Mr. M, and in some half-conscious sense Mr. B knows this. He has noted Mr. M's natural circumspection and care in speaking and has expressed it in a metaphor implying mild criticism.

This description by Mr. B raises, however, the general issue of the "theme of the machine." To control oneself with mechanical precision is a positive value for Mr. B, and his comment therefore implies a covert acknowledgment of Mr. M's power while it converts him from a living to a nonliving thing. In this indirect, metaphorical sense, Mr. B "kills" his instructor and—at the same time—notes the instructor's potential for "killing" him with his "gears" and "mechanical voice." After all, Mr. B is not operating this "machine."

The "machines" in the literature essays are the guns and, in (5), the car. But it would be wrong to interpret the guns and the shooting as the operation of machines. They are guns, instruments of murder and of intention, and they are described that way in every one of the literature essays: there is no ambiguity or vagueness about how the guns are used or when a shooting would occur, and there is no abstract admiration of their mechanical quality. They are, rather, a natural part of one's repertoire of social behaviors, and they appear in the language with just this fluency. Mr. B accepts the customary "literary" license and "rubs out" imaginary people without hesitation or misgiving. At the same time the gun itself is important—it is the formula for self-protection, and it, like the car, is the means for enacting one's will with dispatch.

To be the inventor of thirteen unnamed, though admired, objects is a *translation* of this trancendental will and its instrument. When in the world of social reality—where the task and purpose (in this course) is self-presentation in language—the affective world is altogether translated, and Mr. B speaks a "different language." But his translation, like others of the more familiar sort, is "not faithful." As a result, he expresses his gaining experience of our common environment as knowing the "solid, liquid, and gases" of the earth. In this essay people are referred to only as "others." Flying, traveling, and scuba diving are described as "tools" to "observe the earth." Mr. B's "amazing ability" to invent objects supplies his credentials for admission to society, but in society he "didn't know what to do with" the objects. Yet guns have just the opposite role: they are the natural instruments of the most authentic wishes. In the literature essays, guns are part of the language—that is, certain people just "should be shot" or, as in his error in (2), "shot on his merry way," where the idea of shooting is superimposed on Mr. B's knowledge of the phrase "send on his merry way."

It was not possible, on reading the experience essays, to discern what Mr. B's problem was. We instructors sensed that something was amiss, but we were hesitant to fix on some kind of lack, such as poor training in high school, to explain what would ordinarily be called a failure of diction, poor choice of words, careless spelling, and lack of editing or rewriting. It did not even occur to Mr. M that the experience essays were simply not telling the truth, since this hypothesis would imply a very strong conclusion about Mr. B himself (and one that turned out to be true).

It is likely that most of the experience essays were fantasies, but to Mr. B, as to all other students, *they represented the self that appears in public:* they were his *reality.* We are concerned here not with whether his reality corresponds to ours, but with the relation between the language used in describing "my experience" and that used in describing "imaginary experience." Whatever may have been troubling Mr. B as an individual, he used *two categories of language,* just as did other students in whose work the difference was less easily observable.

These two categories form a *syntactic interdependence* in that each may be used as either the subject or the predicate in the schematic formulation (for example) "tool means gun" or "gun means tool." The syntactic reversibility corresponds to a reversibility of motivation as Mr. B shifts between contexts of social functioning. Thus one context is "telling my class about myself," and the other is "telling my class my experience of the literature." The conception of the "literary world" is an objectification of the individual's emotional and affective language options where *intentionality* originates. When Mr. B creates the immediate intention of, say, telling the class about his inventions, in response to the "assigned" question and to the need for affirmative self-presentation, the intentionality operates as a concealed principle of language guidance and translates the diminished sense of self into an exaggerated sense: "You are a genious." In writing about the stories, the intentionality operates in the *same way*—"I would like to shoot certain people"—except that the convention of the otherness of the imaginary world dissociates the writer's articulation of his wishes from himself. Our legitimate option to cancel this convention permits us to perceive the language as a function of the underlying intentionality.

Any language instance is a function of both the intention and the intentionality. The problem has been to find a systematic means of deciding how, in each instance, each is to be understood. In the foregoing case, the solution has been to rely on the language formulations given "about" reading experiences just because the "otherness" convention of literature is cancelable. However, relative to the individual, the two categories of language are intrinsically reversible in any "meaning" predication: the literature essays "mean" the experience essays *and* the experience essays "mean" the literature essays. The reversibility means that one category cannot be understood by itself. It is just as impossible to "read" a person's language from seeing only the literature essays as it is from seeing the experience essays alone, even though one has suspicions and makes guesses from seeing just one category. Only when both categories are available can one see the relation between intention and intentionality in either one. And then it is only through negotiation with the writer that one can claim a reasonable authority for understanding the language system of the person at that time.

The intersubjective conception of language entails a series of syntactical interdependencies between intention and intentionality, between historical self-presentation and literary self-presentation, between psychological purpose and social purpose. These interdependencies govern and appear in any single instance of language use, from the word to the book. Disclosing and understanding them, however, *requires an intersubjective context,* such as the classroom, where deliberate procedures are undertaken that govern each individual's action in the same way. This context makes the language meaningful itself, and at the same time renders the disclosure of meaning possible, pragmatic, and pertinent to some real intersubjective purpose.

The traditional, familiar problem of "literature and composition" is just one aspect of language that might be illuminated by this conception of language. Any other enterprise presenting its findings in language is amenable to understanding in these terms. But even from the seemingly local perspective of the professional problem in "English," I think that nothing less than a new conception of language will be adequate.

6   Literature, Composition, and the Structure of English

Nancy R. Comley and Robert Scholes

We propose to analyze the structure of English studies in a new way that will reveal the sources of many of our problems and to offer, more tentatively, a report on some attempts to solve these problems with specific curricular and pedagogical remedies. The structure we propose to discuss is a kind of deep structure or, better yet, an unconscious one, shaped by the interactions of our needs and the repressive situations in which we find ourselves. Like the Freudian unconscious, it manifests itself in irregularities, in slips, allowing us to speak of a psychopathology of everyday English teaching.

This hidden structure reveals itself most obviously in certain inconsistencies of speech and action. If a woman from Venus (we are tired of the proverbial "man from Mars") were to come among us and select a native informant from one of our English departments, she would discover that in English departments we believe we are teaching two things, which we usually call "literature" and "composition." These two entities appear to be totally unrelated except that both involve the English language. In fact, they are connected within the "field" of English by a mytho-logical structure that can be brought to light by analysis in much the way that structuralist and poststructuralist critics like Claude Lévi-Strauss and Roland Barthes analyze the workings of mythologies in both "primitive" and "civilized" cultures.

The field of English is organized by two primary gestures of differentiation, dividing and redividing the field by binary opposition. First of all, we divide the field into two categories: literature and nonliterature. This is, of course, an invidious distinction. That is, we mark those texts labeled literature as good or important and dismiss nonliterary texts as beneath our notice. This division is traversed and supported by another, which is just as important, though somewhat less visible. We distinguish between the production and the consumption of texts, and, as might be expected in a society like ours, we privilege consumption over production, just as the larger culture privileges the consuming class over the producing class.[1]

One further distinction and our basic structure will be complete. This is the most obvious, the most problematic, and therefore perhaps the most important. We distinguish between what is "real" and what is "academic" to our own disadvantage. At some level we accept the myth of the ivory tower and secretly despise our own activities as trivial unless we can link them to a "reality" outside academic life. Thus we may consume "literature," which comes from outside our classrooms, but we cannot produce literature in classes, nor can we teach its production. Instead, we teach something called "creative writing"—the production of pseudoliterary texts.

The proper consumption of literature we call "interpretation," and teaching this skill, like displaying it in academic papers, articles, and books, is our greatest glory. Producing literature is regarded as beyond us, to the point where even those writers who are hired by academies to teach creative writing are felt to dwindle into academics themselves, and we suspect that their work may only be creative writing too. How often are the works of the faculty of the Iowa Writers Workshop studied in the classrooms of the Iowa English Department?

The consumption of nonliterature can be taught. It is called "reading," and most college and university English departments are content to hope it has been dealt with in secondary school— a hope that seems less and less well founded as we go on. But actual nonliterature is perceived as grounded in the realities of existence, where it is produced in response to personal or socio-economic imperatives and therefore justifies itself functionally. By its very usefulness, its nonliterariness, it eludes our grasp. It

1. In a discussion of the differences between literary and composition research, Paula Johnson makes a similar distinction: "Student texts are not merely there, waiting to be studied; they are elicited in order to be improved. That distinction, I shrewdly suspect, is one of the forces that will keep the gap between literature and composition yawning, despite the potency of the new theoretical paradigm to close it. Literary scholarship does not strive to effect anything, except maybe an advancement in academic rank for the scholar. Composition research, on the other hand, tries to do something to what it studies. The social analogue is plain: the leisured elite and the rude mechanicals." "Writing Programs and the English Department," *Profession '80* (New York: Modern Language Association, 1980), 15.

can be read but not interpreted, because it supposedly lacks those secret/hidden/deeper meanings so dear to our pedagogic hearts. Nor can it be produced when cut off from the exigencies of its real situations. What *can* be produced within the academy is an unreal version of it, "pseudononliterature," which is indeed produced in an appalling volume. We call the production of this stuff "composition."

The structure of English as a field can then be diagramed in the following simple manner:

PRODUCTION	TEXTS	CONSUMPTION
	literature	interpretation
creative writing	pseudoliterature	
	nonliterature	
composition	pseudononliterature	

This diagram operates for most of us as a semiconscious mental construct, manifesting itself concretely in our departmental behavior, including curriculum design, teaching assignments, and economic rewards. Both an ideology and a hierarchy are captured in this scheme. The greatest value is placed upon the things in the top categories, and the least upon the things at the bottom. In many English departments we can find sexual and economic structures mapped upon this value system, with higher-paid, predominantly male faculty members at the top and their lower-paid, predominantly female colleagues at the bottom.

What to Do?

For many teachers the proper response to this situation is simply inversion of the hierarchy. Since composition is in demand, let the "law" of supply and demand work until composition replaces interpretation at the top of the heap. Fortunately or unfortunately, things don't work this way. The demand for more composition courses operates *within* a larger economic system as well as within the prestige system that privileges literature and its interpreters. As long as the prestige system is in place, the social and economic structures of English departments will align themselves with it. Even if it were a good idea, the hierarchy could not be inverted. But it is not a good idea.

The proper remedy for our troubles must begin with the deconstruction of our basic system of binary oppositions itself. The whole purpose of laying bare a structure such as this is achieved only when we succeed in deconstructing it. Ultimately, the opposition between literature and composition must be broken down. And to accomplish this we must break down all the lesser oppositions that support the great one. Here is a brief sketch of how that may be done theoretically, followed by some examples of how it may be done in classroom practice.

1. Literature/nonliterature. Under pressure from structuralists and poststructuralists, this distinction has already been seriously called into question. Without developing each point, let us list some of the cogent critiques of this binary opposition. First, any fragment of any text may be brought within the body of an avowedly literary text: the most banal speech or writing may appear in a novel as an aspect of characterization or setting, to great literary effect. Second, all texts have secret/hidden/deeper meanings, and none more so than the supposedly obvious and straightforward productions of journalists, historians, and philosophers. Finally, we all know that many texts that are formally literary (i.e., look like poems, plays, or stories) are of less interest than many other texts that are cast in an explanatory, meditative, or expository form. The "great books" are not all belletristic, and if belletrism falls, then any text may be studied in an English course. And who is to say that Locke or Gibbon is less valuable than Dryden or Gray? The literature/nonliterature distinction cannot survive a critique that succeeds in separating literariness from value, yet that is precisely what all the formal and structural studies of the past decades have enabled us to do.

2. Production/consumption. Taken in the form in which they present themselves to us, these terms are equivalent to writing and reading. The way out of our dilemma here is, first, to perceive reading not simply as consumption but as a productive activity, the making of meaning, in which one is guided by the text one reads, of course, but not simply manipulated by it; and, second, to perceive writing as an activity that is also guided and sustained by prior texts. The writer is always reading and the reader is always writing. The student who produces a written "reading"

of a text is our paradigm here; she is, of course, both a writer and a reader. The student who reads the "world" and writes about it is also sustained by other texts while producing her interpretation of whatever things or states of affairs are being considered. Some written readings are more productive than others, or more creative, but this is *never* simply a matter of the form taken by the text produced.

3. Real world/academy. This is the subtlest and most pernicious distinction, rising again and again to challenge us. Schools have been functioning as a preparation for something that "commences" as schooling ends, but this state of affairs is not given to us as a part of the nature of things. We have drifted into thinking of our lives as marked by stages that are sharply divided from one another. This has not always been so in our tradition. Men as well as boys walked alongside the peripatetic philosophers. There are signs, now, that these rigid chronological distinctions may be losing force. Even Yale University has finally decided that adults may actually be educable.

It can be argued that study and work may be performed by the same person at the same stage of life but that they are still not the same thing; and this is true—up to a point. But one who studies in order to publish new discoveries and receive financial rewards for them is in the "real" world, is she not? Or is her world real only if she seeks to minimize the effort and maximize the profit? And what of one who studies to improve her own mind? This improved mind becomes the goal and product of the labor, and any actual texts produced are then evidence of this other, invisible product. Is an improved mind real? Is it marketable?

I think we must answer these last questions affirmatively. Something real is going on inside academies, but the method of this real production has much artifice in it. Students as a class may be defined by their involvement in what Erving Goffman has called "practicings."

> In our society, and probably in all others, capacity to bring off an activity as one wants to—ordinarily defined as the possession of skills—is very often developed through a kind of utilitarian make-believe. The purpose of this practicing is to give the neophyte experience in performing under conditions in which (it is felt) no actual engagement with the world is allowed, events here having been "decoupled" from their usual embedment in consequentiality. Presumably muffing or

failure can occur both economically and instructively. What one has here are dry runs, trial sessions, run-throughs—in short, "practicings."[2]

There is a difference between practice and earnest, which we must acknowledge. We err only when we make the gesture of erecting this difference into two "worlds," one of which is held to be all practice, the other all earnest. The neophyte drill press operator must practice, too, before being given real projects. More important for our purposes, however, is that all who write, whether in an ivy-covered study or a crowded office, are involved in a process that moves from practice to earnest, beginning with dry runs, trial sessions, rough drafts, scratching out, and crumpled sheets in the wastebasket. There is, then, something inescapably academic about all writing, whether in school or out, and many a text begun in school has finished out in the world. The "real" and the "academic" deeply interpenetrate.

In theory, it is not only possible but easy to deconstruct the system of oppositions that supports the split between literature and composition. But what can we do in our real daily academic lives to dismantle the practices in which we are enmeshed and replace them with better ones? Here we must all respond in terms of the situations in which we find ourselves. The aim is to devise a curriculum that breaks down in a practical way these pernicious oppositions we have been discussing. This means new courses and new types of assignment, devised within the framework of what is possible at a given school at a given time. We do not presume to offer a master (or mistress) plan for all courses at all institutions. Instead we shall discuss in some detail things that can be done—that *have* been done—to deconstruct the opposition between literature and composition at the point where it is most powerfully felt: the freshman English course.

Traditionally, the solution to devising a proper freshman English course has been based on one extreme or another. Either we introduce "literary" texts into the curriculum, which leads to the inevitable drift toward interpretation as the focus of all energies, or we resolutely purge literature in the name of some pure ideal of expository or functional writing. But functional writing removed from its "usual embedment in consequentiality" is only pseudofunctional; and literary texts may be used for many things

2. Erving Goffman, *Frame Analysis* (New York: Harper and Row, 1974), 59.

other than interpretive consumption. The pseudofunctional is already in the realm of artifice. Moreover, the literary text may be a pre-text for all sorts of responses. The bases for our necessary deconstruction are already at hand. We have only to learn how to use them.

The first step in arriving at a new approach to freshman English is to locate the qualities of good writing that are shared by "literary" and "nonliterary" texts. There are many such qualities that most of us could agree on: clarity, power, precision, originality, convincingness, coherence, correctness (to name some that cover different aspects of the writing process). Any staff will benefit from discussing these matters, and a staff that has reached agreement on a set of virtues can devise an arrangement of readings and writings that will point toward them. For purposes of illustration here, we will discuss a single "virtue" or complex of qualities that can be expressed on one word: "voice."

Voice in writing is a function of coherence or consistency, among other things. It suggests a person behind the words, whose personality is one focus of organization. Voice also suggests the presence of the receiver of a text, a reader or "listener" also conceived in human terms. Finally, voice suggests a consistent attitude toward the subject under discussion. Unvoiced prose is marked by diffuseness and dullness. Voiced prose will be both more focused and livelier. Voicing is a major quality of successful writing, whether in traditional literary forms or in texts usually thought of as nonliterary. Even the sociological prose of Goffman, quoted above, is strongly marked by an individual voice.

In freshman English, voice is a special problem—often because students have undergone prior training designed to purge them of all impulses toward individuality. Voicelessness is a major feature of pseudononliterary discourse. And this problem is often compounded by previous experience of "creative writing," where students are encouraged to believe that "free" composition will necessarily express valuable facets of their unique and precious personalities. But selfhood must be achieved by an effort of expression. It is not given but earned, and one of the ways we earn it is by trying out different voices and learning the limits of what they can express.

In helping students achieve voices in prose, we have found lyric poetry especially useful. The short, accessible modern poem is often a reservoir of compositional techniques. Such poems easily command interest and attention, and they reward such attention. If we take away their privileges as sacred literary objects to be interpreted, they prove immensely functional as generators of controlled, voiced student writing. We will close this essay by discussing some actual examples of encounters between students and poems in freshman English classes at the University of Oklahoma.

We can begin by examining the case of Betsy (not her real name), an attractive, intelligent young woman who always made A's in her high-school English courses. She is representative of the majority of freshmen at the University of Oklahoma who have taken college preparatory courses in high school. Her first writing assignment in freshman English was to describe a place that was special to her. This writing assignment followed the reading and discussion of a text in this mode—in this case an excerpt from Nikki Giovanni's "Knoxville Revisited"—in which a personal voice and viewpoint are strongly present. It would not be easy to assign Giovanni's essay to either of the traditional categories; it is on the border between literature and nonliterature. Betsy's response to this assignment was depressing to read, as were most others in the class. Because these students had been forbidden to use "I" and "you" in their high school writing, their essays sounded as if the writers came from a strange world where life was lived in the passive voice, and where no one had an identity, an experiencing self. Here are a couple of examples of the struggle they were having. The first is from Betsy's paper, the second from her classmate Gary's attempt to describe his old neighborhood:

> As one creeps down the street, cars packed bumper to bumper, the senses are bombarded by a variety of sights and sounds.

> Many summer days were spent scaling this tree and one day in particular was filled with the fear of falling and breaking my ankle.

What Gary was trying to say was that he did fall out of the tree and break his ankle, a fact that came clear in a subsequent revision after he and the rest of the class had been reassured again and again that it was all right to use "I." Such anxiety had of course made it very difficult for these students to write. In a later assignment, Betsy's description of her previous writing experience reveals the cause of this anxiety and the difficulty students like her had in writing about their own experiences.

Although some high schools do have college preparatory classes, many of these, the finest example being in my high school, "Preparation for Language Arts in College," have done more harm than good. PLA, as this class was lovingly referred to, taught the college-bound senior all the essential writing skills and rules necessary for freshman English courses. The strict "flunk-if-you-use-the-first-person-pronoun five paragraph" essay was the major focal point of the class—the highlight being we were allowed to turn in five of these a semester. Not only did this type of writing cut off all creative thinking, it most effectively produced a mass of duplicate essays with the only change being the substitution of required topics: Drug Abuse, Alcoholism, and Women in the Draft, to name a few of the more original ones.

To relieve the monotony, we developed various, simple, yet highly effective systems of completing these assignments. In most cases, a friend and I would alternate in making up every other sentence so that inevitably our papers would turn out to be exact replicas, with only minor changes used, such as the subject-verb switch or the turned-around-transition play. It was almost a challenge to see if the teacher would notice the similarities. As expected, she never did.

Betsy and her classmates were adept at pseudononliterary discourse, but it was the only discourse they knew. The fact that neither she nor most of her classmates had responded to the strong voice of Nikki Giovanni and been able to use it as a model signaled another problem: they did not know how to read. Their previous experiences with literature had been as bad as their previous experience with writing. They had read stories and plays and been quizzed on the questions following the selections in their anthologies. They had read very little poetry because it was rarely taught. And because it was rarely taught, they assumed it was difficult to read and understand. All the more reason, then, to confront them with poetry to see whether its strangeness would help break down the barriers of the pseudodiscourse they had learned so well.

For the next assignment the class read and discussed E. A. Robinson's "Richard Cory," Gwendolyn Brooks's "We Real Cool," and Robert Creeley's "Oh No." Betsy chose to work on

"Richard Cory." The assignment required her to write from Richard Cory's point of view, to recreate his thought just before he put a bullet through his head. Her response signaled the beginning of her breakout from the constraints of pseudodiscourse:

As Richard Cory slowly looked around the room, he memorized for the last time the objects representing his life. The head of a lion above the fireplace, its mouth open in a silent roar of defiance, the skin of a bear sprawled on the floor, the antlers of various deer and antelope scattered throughout the room, all reminded him of hunting trips with his father. The mahogany desk, once covered with his father's important papers was bare—the dust clearly visible to the naked eye. He detected the distinct, yet subtle touches of a woman—the flower arrangements, once alive with color and fragrance, now dried and brittle, the embroidered pillows on the sofa and loveseat gave evidence of hours of utmost care and patience. He pictured his father, with his ever-present pipe in one hand, boasting about some trophy acquired anywhere from South Africa to Alaska. In his mind, he saw his mother with her easel sitting in the corner working on the painting she had been doing ever since he could remember.

That was before it happened. He remembered the day he had been told of the plane crash that killed both of his parents. He had never fully been able to accept the fact. He was dead inside—oblivious to the happenings going on around him. Each day was the same—a routine he had been trained to follow. But as he walked over to the desk and pulled the pistol out of the drawer, a rare smile played about his lips because he knew everything would be all right—for soon he would be with his parents.

When asked about her experience writing—specifically, what happened to produce such a good response, she replied, "I liked the poem, and I was able to get inside his head. I could see what he saw, and I wrote it down."

The poem had provided her with a structure and a voice. She was beginning to develop her own voice by assuming a role; her audience was not the teacher, but rather the townspeople in the poem, for she was filling that narrative gap in the poem between those who work and "wish that we were in his place," and Richard Cory. She had produced an imaginative, creative interpretation of the poem and in so doing had fulfilled a composition assignment. The structure of the poem had allowed her creative freedom by giving her rules to guide her in writing. She had learned more about point of view, and she had had practice in descriptive narrative discourse. Equally, if not more, important, she had discovered that writing could be pleasurable. She had also discovered that poetry was not intimidating, and that it spoke eloquently and directly to her about life. She had seen in the condensed richness of the poem the story of a man's life as told by his neighbors, and had responded to the mystery of Richard Cory's suicide. Because the poem was part of a writing assignment, she had taken the first steps in interpretation by substituting a prose structure for the poetic structure so as to "translate" the poem into a narrative. She then took another interpretive step in asking questions about the mystery in the poem: Why did Richard Cory put a bullet through his head? What does the poem suggest as a reason for this action? Who is speaking in the poem? To whom? She did not provide a sophisticated interpretation of the poem, but she had considered the basic questions any literary critic would ask, and her response shows sensitivity, a quality necessary to any good critical reader.

Before the first semester was over, Betsy had developed into a more confident writer and reader. Like Janet Emig's case study Lynn in *The Composing Processes of Twelfth-Graders,* Betsy was bright and eager to please, so she learned quickly. Unlike Lynn, who avoided expressing herself, Betsy was eager to do so. The use of intertexts whose structures set up rules of role and audience but at the same time gave her creative freedom helped her to develop her own voice.

Students like Betsy are easy and pleasant to work with. The real challenge in teaching freshman composition comes from those students with less advantaged backgrounds than Betsy's, who populate our basic writing sections. These students, whose ACT scores range from 7 to 18, have usually had very little previous writing experience and have a variety of remedial problems. But because their previous education had not indoctrinated them into rigid patterns for "success in college," they were more receptive than their college-track peers to writing assignments that were very different from the workbook-type English they had been subjected to in high school. We had used Gwendolyn Brooks's "We Real Cool" (see Appendix A) in both regular and basic sections of freshman composition to generate reflective writing. Students were asked to assume the role of one of the pool players at the Golden Shovel twenty years later. They were to decide what had happened in those twenty years, who they were now, and how they saw their youthful selves. Most students enjoyed this assignment and had little trouble with it. Reports from teachers in both regular and basic sections noted a marked development of voice and a stronger sense of audience than in previous work. Another improvement for many students who had been unable to generate much writing at all was in content. This latter development was most significant among basic writers.

For them, "We Real Cool" offered rich possibilities. They were fascinated with its syntax and its jazzy beat. They also noted that if they had used such sentence structure in a composition they would have been criticized for it: "vary your sentence structure" had appeared all too frequently on their high-school papers. But what if you combined some of these sentences and made them more grammatical? The assignment was to combine each pair of the four pairs of sentences in the poem, making four sentences of two clauses related by an appropriate connective and adding as few words as possible to make these sentences complete and correct. They then combined the four sentences into two, and finally, the two into one sentence. After they had worked with this exercise, they discovered that if they had succeeded syntactically and grammatically, they had lost the poem: they had taken away the condensed syntax and rhythmic beat that give the poem its voice—its poeticalness, if you will. They were learning something about poetry by playing with it, and one student, noting that the 1950s sociolect was a bit dated, produced a 1980s version for "extra credit":

We Real Live!

The Students
Seven in Mrs. Merz Class

We real live. We
give five. We

party long. We
fight strong. We

smoke weed. We
take speed. (We

study too.) We
dress GQ. We

mellow in May. We
are here to stay.

The students in Mrs. Merz's class liked working with poetry and went on to more complex assignments, such as comparing Brueghel's *Landscape with the Fall of Icarus* with William Carlos Williams's "The Fall of Icarus" and W. H. Auden's "Musée des Beaux Arts." Some of these students later elected second-semester basic writing sections that used poetry for all writing assignments.

The condensed richness and complexity of poetry, its appeal to both the emotions and the intellect, make it stimulating to work with. A writing approach to literary texts, in which students write in the forms they are reading or use such texts as intertexts for writing in other forms, not only will improve their ability to write in all forms of discourse, but will also improve ability to read and interpret texts.

These modest examples, drawn from the many in our files, are in no way exceptional. This sort of evidence is meant not to be persuasive in itself, but to suggest what may be achieved by bringing poetry and composition together in the classroom without the preconceptions that usually accompany them. When students are not obliged to consume poems by interpretation but are free to produce new texts based on the poems as pre-texts, they add the energy built into the poems to their own. And when they write in highly structured situations, but unconstrained by the parameters of the five-paragraph theme or the algorithms of functional prose, their competence grows along with their commitment to the enterprise. What they produce is neither "creative writing" nor "composition," in the usual sense of those expressions, but simply writing—writing that illustrates their growing command of this essential skill. These results can be replicated in any classroom.

At the end of *A Portrait of the Artist as a Young Man,* Stephen Dedalus is persuaded that he can escape his Irish religion and nationality by voyaging to Paris. In *Ulysses* a sadder and wiser Stephen taps his brow and says, "In here it is that I must kill the priest and the king." Less dramatically but no less significantly, we must destroy our own mental idols if we are to escape the idolatry of English under which we now labor. The simple but important classroom victories described here depend upon our rethinking those fundamental oppositions by which we have defined ourselves and our work for so long. As Thomas Kuhn has shown us in the physical sciences, a sense of crisis usually precedes a shift in paradigms. We have the sense of crisis, all right. Let us get on to the new paradigm.

Appendix A

"We Real Cool"
Gwendolyn Brooks

The Pool Players
Seven at the Golden Shovel

We real cool. We
Left school. We

Lurk late. We
Strike straight. We

Sing sin. We
Thin gin. We

Jazz June. We
Die soon.[3]

3. From Gwendolyn Brooks, *The World of Gwendolyn Brooks,* copyright © 1959 by Gwendolyn Brooks. Reprinted by permission of Harper and Row, publishers.

Maps and Genres
Exploring Connections in the Arts and Sciences

Elaine P. Maimon

Individuals trained in literary criticism tend to map the genres in the way a famous *New Yorker* cover maps the world. Saul Steinberg, the cover artist, adopts the global perspective of a typical resident of Manhattan. So we see a detailed street map of Manhattan, Sixth Avenue, Seventh Avenue, Eighth Avenue. Then, slightly to the left, we find Chicago, and in close proximity San Francisco and Japan. The literary genres are our Manhattan streets. We know them intimately. In fact, when we think of genre studies, we think of fiction, poetry, and drama. Somewhere not too far from our immediate attention—in Chicago or San Francisco—is the informal, belletristic essay of Charles Lamb, E. B. White, and George Orwell. And on the periphery of our understanding— near foreign and industrialized Japan—are vast uncharted regions, nonfiction prose and technical writing, which subsume all genres recommended by our colleagues in other disciplines.

As literary critics, we indicate our attitude toward nonfiction prose even by the label we give it. We define this broad area of discourse—the area that encompasses most of what our colleagues in other disciplines do—by a negative: nonfiction prose. We demonstrate thereby some disrespect for communities removed from our own, because we lump all their distinct prose forms under this imprecise label. What are the territorial and cultural boundaries in this vast uncharted realm?

Potentially, literary scholars have the ability to map the genres more precisely, although the land of the lab report may seem far off indeed. And if we look closely at our capacity for generic mapping, we may find other highly cultivated understandings that we have derived from our literary studies and that we can effectively draw upon to make ourselves better scholars and teachers of composition. We can bridge the gap between literature and composition by seeing ourselves as scholars of language, but our professional experience has in many ways socialized us to deny this potential even when connections should be apparent.

The purpose of this chapter is to highlight connections within English studies and between English and other disciplines in the arts and sciences. Extending our theory of genre can help us examine the way various disciplines have developed traditions that shape the reading and writing of their practitioners. To understand and use these genres is to show membership in the community that has evolved these forms.

Thinking in Genres, Writing in Genres

A theory of genre defines the terms of the relationship between reader and writer, speaker and listener. Readers and writers are partners, just as reading and writing, speaking and listening are connected, interactive processes. We can understand the importance of generic considerations most clearly from instances of failed communication. If a scholar at a cocktail party were to respond to an inquiry by presenting a classroom lecture, communication would fail because of genre confusion. Given the more conservative and conventional nature of writing, generic considerations are even more important in writing than in speech. If we begin to read something that we expect to be a short story when it is actually a case study, we will badly misinterpret the piece until we revise our perception of the genre. Just so, if we wish to write a case study but our only generic models are short stories, we will fail to communicate with readers of case studies.

The forms of writing within a particular intellectual community manifest modes of thinking within that community. A lyric poet learns to behave like a lyric poet by reading and hearing lyric poetry. When the poet writes his own lyric poem, he creates something that never existed before but that bears a family resemblance to other lyric poems. Without that family resemblance and the mannerisms that go with it, the piece of writing is anomalous and communication is at risk, unless we can identify a resemblance to another family.

We can understand something of the poet's perspective by looking closely at the manifestations of that perspective in lyric poetry. Other genres reveal the modes of thinking of people who write within those forms. A broad and inclusive study of genre, a study that is not confined to literary forms, can help us understand the thinking processes of writers who use those forms. A genre is more than a bundle of conventional details about the spacing of words on the page, footnote format, and other arbitrary matters. The configurations that form our surface definition of genre have a heuristic potential. Through a study of genre in all disciplines in the arts and sciences, we can learn more about the varieties of thinking in the academy and in the larger world of professional and public activity. Most important, by studying the full range of academic prose, we can better understand the traditions of liberal learning in the arts and sciences.

Such a study should not lead us to teach blind conformity to a set of arbitrary conventions tacitly understood by colleagues in other fields. Those of us who specialize in the analysis of discourse know that the better a writer understands the conventions of a particular genre, the more creative that writer can be in breaking the rules for effect. The poet who breaks the rules of a Petrarchan sonnet does so out of a deep respect for and understanding of the sonnet tradition. Too often, we encourage scientists to write poems instead of lab reports out of a sense of deep disdain for the tradition of report writing. I am suggesting an engaged yet objective analysis of a wide variety of generic forms as a way to encourage students to understand the concept of verbal traditions. Once science students learn to regard the lab report as a genre, they may be better prepared to identify other verbal constraints in other genres. And if science students understand the conventions of a lab report, some may be prepared to be adventuresome within these constraints and by so doing experience the possibilities of verbal play.

Conventions are expectations in the minds of readers. Readers who are members of the same intellectual community share these expectations because of a history of common experiences. Some people learn these conventions effortlessly; others, usually those who have not read extensively in the particular genres under consideration, need much more explicit instruction.

Stanley Fish writes of "the authority of interpretive communities." Fish says that we recognize a poem when we see one—or, by extension, a lab report or a case study or an assignment—because we belong to an interpretive community that shares the same recipe for constructing these texts.[1] Genre conventions are

1. Stanley Fish, *Is There a Text in This Class? The Authority of Interpretive Communities* (Cambridge: Harvard University Press, 1980), 14.

constructed by a community that has practiced writing particular kinds of texts. In all disciplines texts are made, not decoded.

As literary critics we can explore the generic conventions of other interpretive subcommunities in the arts and sciences. Because English instructors are accustomed to posing generic questions, I am proposing that we can, with just a little help from our friends in other disciplines, make explicit the tacit conventions of a variety of genres. In fact, our own role as fellow explorers, rather than experts, may even win over our students to share more enthusiastically our new generic explorations. We do not have to teach the social or natural sciences in order to help our students understand genres within these fields.

Let us explore briefly the conventions of the lab report, a generic example that seems particularly foreign to literary critics. After reading a few successful laboratory reports, we can see that this genre manifests particular conventions of voice, form, and audience (and we are the ones who use such metalinguistic terms, not our colleagues in the sciences).

The voice in a lab report sounds an impersonal tone, which expresses the scientist's particular stance on experience. Scientific writing gives visible form to the scientific method: the systematic formulation and testing of hypotheses. Scientists perform rituals to establish distance between themselves and the material they are studying. The conventions of report writing are in a sense theatrical techniques to help scientists maintain the objective stance.

Scientists often use the passive voice as one way of communicating their distance from their material. Not all passive constructions are equally effective, however. The following construction is an inappropriate and ineffective use of the passive:

The radish seed was germinated on filter paper.

Most scientists would prefer the following active construction:

The radish seed germinated on filter paper.

The passive in the first example is superfluous, although the two constructions are equally impersonal. On the other hand, most scientists would probably prefer the following passive construction to the active one written below it:

Passive
The total percentage of the seeds germinating and the average time to germinate were measured for each sample.

Active
I measured the total percentage of the seeds germinating and the average time to germinate for each sample.

Some scientists, however, would find the following active, third-person version acceptable or even preferable to the passive:

Active, third person
The experimenter measured the total percentage of the seeds germinating and the average time to germinate each sample.

The point is to maintain the impersonal tone by keeping the biographical human figure at some distance from the natural phenomena he is measuring. When scientists perform as scientists, they pretend to divest themselves of human biases and inhibitions. The best scientific writers are the best actors; they understand the complexities of the scientific role.

The form of the lab report also reflects the scientist's disengaged stance on experience. The typical lab report is divided into seven sections:

1. Title
2. Abstract
3. Introduction
4. Methods and Materials
5. Results
6. Conclusions
7. References Cited

The introduction is a short expository essay that presents an overview of relevant research. The methods and materials section is characterized by both description and narration. The results section includes description, narration, and exposition, with the verbal material almost always supplemented by graphic representations: tables and figures. The section entitled conclusions presents in expository form an analysis of the results, along with a discussion of the wider significance of the material. Anything resembling persuasion would be a violation of generic constraints. Scientists present their findings; they do not argue for them. They might say that the current experiment does not replicate the findings of Brown et al., but they probably will not say that the current experiment repudiates Brown et al.

In a lab report subdivisions and subheadings are essential to the genre. Scientists know that their readers will probably not read the whole experiment and will instead focus on the relevant parts. Readers are assumed to be other scientists who are interested in seeing how the reported experiment advances scientific knowledge. Some readers may wish to replicate the experiment, so precise reporting is essential. They may want to check references to the pertinent work of other scientists, so they need the names of those scientists and the dates of their work. The author/ date reference form should not be interpreted as a quirk that scientists adopt to separate themselves from humanists. The MLA footnote form is appropriate to readers who want to check quotations in the appropriate edition of an author's work. Direct quotations are rarely used in the lab report genre. As a consequence, MLA form is not so useful to scientists.

When scientists read within the lab report genre, they have expectations that they do not bring to nonscientific writing. Scientists do not wish to be amused when reading laboratory reports. A catchy title like "How Much Salt Can a Radish Take?" would irritate most informed readers of this genre. Humor and flair are not universally appropriate or effective, and in this context they can be distracting. It is not that scientists are by nature cantankerous or humorless people. It is simply that the generic signals of the lab report make cleverness inappropriate, just as a joke at the wrong moment can send a message about the joker's lack of tact. Since generic conventions pertain to knowledgeable behavior within a defined context, each genre has its own serious faux pas. A scientist who writes, "The data indicates" instead of "The data indicate" is not simply committing an error in subject/verb agreement, nor is he merely showing ignorance of Latin neuter plural forms. He is telling other scientists that he is inexperienced with data, that he has not worked with or reported many data, and that he is therefore not an experienced member of the scientific community.

Many students will never be practicing scientists and therefore will not be in danger of breaking generic rules and committing these faux pas. Why then should nonscientists study these generic constraints? First, such study expands their understanding of genre as a concept. Second, analyzing and practicing the generic rituals

of a number of communities helps students develop the intellectual mobility of educated people. Certainly, all educated people
can benefit from understanding the traditions of science and the
elegant methods developed to pose questions about the physical
world and then to suggest possible answers based on empirical
investigation. Studying the lab report as a genre will help students
learn how scientists behave. If students are guided in this analysis
by an English teacher, a humanist who is an expert in language,
we may be mapping a new route to connect C. P. Snow's two
worlds.

The emphasis on genre that I have been discussing should not
be misinterpreted as a choice of product over process. I dislike
the assumption held by some composition scholars that product
and process are opposite poles and that one has to choose. Some—
certainly not all—processes are intended to lead to a public and
communicable form. We can learn something about the writer and
about his discipline by looking at that public behavior. We also
need to learn more about those private processes that lead to the
finished product. We can learn something about these hidden processes from protocol analysis, the study of tape recordings writers
make to detail their procedures of composing.[2] Less formally, we
can ask our colleagues in other disciplines to tell us how they go
about their work in the laboratory, in the library, and in the field.
We will find from such inquiry that at every stage the process of
recording and analyzing phenomena reveals not only forms of
behavior that all experienced writers engage in but also distinctive
perspectives on experience shared by a particular scholarly community. The field notebook of an anthropologist, for example, will
record answers to questions that many of us in literature would
rarely think to ask: for example, What is the exact distance between the location of the bones in the Shanidar Cave and the
location of the pollen sample? The anthropologist may ask this
question because he believes materials with pollen content indicate the presence of flowers and therefore of funerary rites and
religion among the Neanderthals.

The anthropologist's preliminary writing manifests his capacity
for critical thinking in his discipline. Critical thinking means mak-

2. Linda Flower and John R. Hayes developed protocol analysis and its applications to written composition. Their procedures are described in the following
article: Linda Flower and John R. Hayes, "A Cognitive Process Theory of Writing," *College Composition and Communication* 32 (December 1981): 365–87.

ing choices, asking the right questions. Students learn how anthropologists think by learning the kinds of preliminary questions they ask and the answers they write down.

Those of us trained in literary research have long been interested in the process of composition. We have studied writers' manuscripts at various stages; we have read letters and journals to understand writers' evolutionary processes of thought; we have written biographies that explored writers' habits and quirks. That long-standing curiosity about how writers behave helps link our two interests in composition and literature. If we extend that interest to the composing practices of writers outside the literary fields, we will simply be doing something familiar in a less familiar realm. Not only will such study extend scholarship, it will enhance our teaching of composition.

Teaching Genres in the Composition Course

A required composition course should be an introduction to composing academic discourse in the arts and sciences. Since literary scholars are accustomed to addressing questions about discourse, about the composing process that creates it, and about the genres that guide its creation, they are potentially best equipped to teach such a course or to train others to teach it. But we must revise the conventional syllabus for the composition course so that it helps students enter the larger community of academic and public conversation.

The difficulty with most freshman theme writing is that the theme as it is usually taught is a genre that exists nowhere outside the composition classroom, though we often claim that writing themes will help students in all their assignments across the disciplines. Likewise, the research paper, as we have customarily taught it, is also sui generis. Let us look at the topic for a typical freshman research paper: capital punishment. How many of us have choked on quotations strung together like sausages, with only the student's cellophane comments in between?

What if we protected ourselves from this dreariness by taking a cross-disciplinary view of the research paper? We could ask students to do research to discover the questions different scholars might ask about capital punishment. Students would find that scholars are interested in various aspects, and that their questions define the particular genre of research for each discipline. The

anthropologist might explore the relationship between capital punishment and other cultural phenomena. The literary critic might
inquire about the role of capital punishment in certain novels by
Dostoevski. The criminologist might ask about the relationship
between the reinstitution of capital punishment and the crime rate
in various states. We need not be anthropologists or criminologists
to help our students understand the aims and attitudes of scholars
in these fields.

We should remind ourselves that questions about purpose and
audience for a writing project precede decisions about whether
to use narrative, descriptive, or expository means to achieve those
ends. Many composition textbooks present what they call "the
modes of discourse" as if they were genres. I have been arguing
that academic genres are defined by various scholarly communities to embody conventions particular to their disciplines. Narration, for example, is used in a number of academic genres, but
in different ways. When scientists write the methods sections of
their lab reports, they are narrating. But that narration looks very
different from the narrative account of Norman Mailer's arrest in
The Armies of the Night.

The emphasis on modes rather than aims and the illustration of
these modes through literary examples have contributed to the
tacit assumptions that inform the teaching of composition in many
English departments. Since composition, until recently, was not
regarded as a field for serious inquiry, few of us examined the
prevailing paradigm. Richard Young describes the overt features
of this paradigm as follows: "the emphasis on the composed product rather than the composing process; the analysis of discourse
into words, sentences, and paragraphs; the classification of discourse into description, narration, exposition, and argument; the
strong concern with usage (syntax, spelling, punctuation) and with
style (economy, clarity, emphasis); the preoccupation with the
informal essay and the research paper; and so on."[3]

This paradigm views writing and reading as entities. Students
are expected to obtain "things" called effective communication
skills. They are supposed to get the first set of things by looking
at a second set of things—narration, exposition, the semicolon.

---

3. Richard E. Young, "Paradigms and Problems," in *Research on Composing,*
ed. Charles R. Cooper and Lee Odell (Urbana, Ill.: National Council of Teachers
of English, 1978), 31.

This focus on entities rather than processes can be illustrated by an analogy to a studio art class—a class, let us say, in pottery. What if the instructor were to bring to class a Grecian urn? What if he then proceeded to lecture brilliantly on its qualities and then asked the apprentice potters in his class to make their own Grecian urns? When a week later the students appear timidly with their misshapen clay pots, the instructor carts home the ugly, heavy things and spends the weekend lamenting: the high schools should do a better job of teaching craftsmanship. Colleagues in other disciplines should require students to practice making well-wrought urns. Finally, the instructor drops each clay pot on the floor and then spends hours pasting it back together—with red Elmer's glue—to show students how they might next time craft something that more nearly resembles a Grecian urn.

Obviously, little clay pots should stay out of the kiln until students learn to work with the soft clay. Students need advice on work in progress. They can learn from their studio classmates as well as from their instructor how to rework a handle or add an appropriate ornament. Most misshapen pots—and most undergraduate papers—look so ugly because they are unfinished, prematurely abandoned by those who never learned procedures for reshaping.

Of course, many people learn to shape a pot or to craft a composition by studying well-wrought urns. Such study has a place in the studio as well as in the lecture hall. Processes, after all, often if not always lead to products, and careful analyses of the best that has been thought and shaped are always valuable. But I am advocating a new perspective on composition—a perspective that is informed by what we know about the processes of composing and about the multiplicity of genres. According to this new paradigm, we would emphasize the composing process that leads to a completed product. We would view a text as a synthesis of words, sentences, and paragraphs. We would see description, narration, exposition, and argument as means to achieve designated purposes for particular audiences. We would regard usage and style as important but not preoccupying, especially not during the early stages of composing. We would present assignments that more realistically model the constraints of writing tasks in a variety of disciplines, deemphasizing the informal essay and adopting a more sophisticated, multidisciplinary approach to the research paper.

Public writing in any discipline is writing that will be assessed by strangers, or by readers who play the role of strangers. During the drafting stage, instructors function as discerning and helpful collaborators. When a final draft is submitted, instructors have obligations beyond their commitment to the student's growth as a writer, because instructors must also hold students to standards appropriate for apprentices in the academic world. Instructors thereby take on the role of strangers by distancing themselves from the writer and by focusing predominantly on the quality of the text. Graded writing, whatever the form, is public writing, according to this definition.

Not all writing should lead to a public product. Writing is a way to learn. Experienced writers also know that writing is not always public but frequently is private, recorded only for oneself. Literary scholars understand that private writing plays an important role in the lives of poets and novelists. The result of James Britton's study of the composing processes of schoolchildren in England should surprise no one who has read literary biographies. Writing expressively for an audience of one is the best way to explore the self and discover what one wants to say.

Some may object that literary writers have a great deal to explore in private writing, whereas undergraduates have very little. Yet every writer, no matter how inexperienced, has intellectual resources, some vast, some small. The human mind is a library. Even a small library is useful if it has a good cataloging system. The goal of private writing, especially for inexperienced students, is to help them gain access to what they already own, so that they might also be encouraged to expand their collections.

Experienced writers are always working to discover what they think, while student writers often seek conformity to an external idea of what someone else wants. A composition course should help students use private writing to discover their own voices. Then, through explanations of various disciplinary genres, students can experiment with different systematic ways of understanding and explaining experience.

When I suggest the use of disciplinary genres as a heuristic device, I am aware that students may at first perceive these generic explorations as more precise instructions for pleasing a teacher. Beginners initially understand much of what we do as leading them toward predetermined meaning. Students come by their immaturity honestly. Our real goal is to initiate beginners into the community of educated people, to lead them from their former assumptions about predetermined knowledge to the riskier and more dissonant environment in which we live. An introductory composition course can exemplify the intellectual range of the community of educated people—a community that we hope our students aspire to join.

Conversation in the Academic Community

Our community is defined by conversation. Richard Rorty in *Philosophy and the Mirror of Nature* says that culture itself is a conversation.[4] Our goal as scholars is to keep the conversation going. Our goal as teachers is to guide students into new communities and to help novices gain an authentic voice in our conversations. We enter a new community when we learn to talk with its citizens. And we learn to talk with them when we understand the generic properties of their conversations.[5]

Rorty emphasizes dialectic, not necessarily because dialectic will lead to the truth, but because it keeps the lines of communication open. Rorty's principles have profound implications for English teachers and scholars. Those of us who teach introductory composition may be the first members of the academic community to initiate students into the dialectic processes that should characterize higher education.

I am not indicting secondary-school education by suggesting that the freshman composition teacher is frequently the first guide to the subtleties and pleasures of the dialectic process. Certainly, students in some elementary and secondary classes are now being introduced to the dialectic process through procedures for collaborative learning. The more that happens, the better students will be prepared for the transition to the college community. But the college community is a special place. The students are older and therefore developmentally ready or about to become ready

4. Richard Rorty, *Philosophy and the Mirror of Nature* (Princeton: Princeton University Press, 1979), 319.

5. I am indebted to Kenneth A. Bruffee for his interpretation of Richard Rorty's work. See Bruffee's "Liberal Education and the Social Justification of Belief," paper delivered at the Conference on Liberal Learning, Old Beliefs/New Practices, sponsored by the Fund for the Improvement of Postsecondary Education, New York, 4 June 1981, 17–19. For practical pedagogic strategies for organizing collaborative learning, see Kenneth A. Bruffee, *A Short Course in Writing,* 2d ed. (Boston: Little, Brown, 1980).

to manipulate abstractions, to communicate through a metalinguistic system, to project from egoism, to understand multiple frames of reference.[6] The college instructor has much greater opportunity to guide students, to draw a map of the liberally educated community.

The English teacher plays a primary role in leading students from the community of the less educated to the community of the culturally literate. We are the ones who can explain the language of the new community. We can also provide our students with systematic instruction and practice for conversing with each other. English instructors can create an environment that simulates that of the academic community at large—a community made distinctive by the lively exchange of ideas.

To create such an environment, we should educate students to respond productively and critically to each other's work in progress. These experiences in collaborative learning help students become socialized into the academic community. Beginners in college are newcomers to our rites and customs. Many enter college valuing sincere expression above all else. Sincerity—the accurate expression of an internal reality—is an important value and should never be lost. But students must grow to value something else as well: the communication of reasoned belief. Students must learn to express ideas coherently and logically, to draw inferences, to suggest analogies, and to refer to appropriate authorities. Liberal education is a process of learning how scholars behave, in the general academic community and in the smaller social groupings of their disciplines.

Within the disciplines, practitioners adhere to somewhat different rules of evidence. Appeal to authority through direct quotation, for example, is more prevalent in the humanities, whereas drawing inferences from disinterested observations is the predominating mode of research in the natural and social sciences. Scholars in different fields favor the genres that best reflect their disciplinary stance on experience. Humanists favor critical analysis and the defense of a thesis, whereas scientists write reports of findings and nonargumentative reviews of research.

Unless students are introduced to the concepts of genre, audience, and situation early in their college careers, they may very well feel baffled or even alienated by the differing expectations

6. Jean Piaget, *Psychology and Epistemology* (New York: Viking Compass, 1972).

that confront them. Students may conclude that instructors vary because of caprice or idiosyncrasy. A newcomer can soon feel estranged and then alienated if no one explains to him the language and customs of the country.

What are the customs of the country? What defines our community of scholars? In 1852 Cardinal Newman described the ideal education for a liberally educated citizen:

> It is the education which gives a man a clear conscious view of his own opinions and judgments, a truth in developing them, an eloquence in expressing them, and a force in urging them. . . . He has a gift which services him in public, and supports him in retirement, without which good fortune is but vulgar and with which failure and disappointment have a charm.[7]

The liberally educated gentleman whom Newman describes above could depend on attaining his "gift" of critical thinking from sources other than his university education. Everything in his social milieu contributed to the intellectual and cultural resources that provided a basis for his sound reasoning and intellectual tact.

Higher education in contemporary America is committed to bringing the resources of liberal learning to a group much wider than the upper-middle-class males who would be educated in Newman's ideal university. For the first time in the history of higher education anywhere, we are striving to bring the liberating possibilities of academic processes to all interested citizens. This unprecedented expansion of postsecondary education in America has been rapid; the land-grant universities of the mid-nineteenth century, the GI Bill following World War II, the community college movement of the late 1950s and early 1960s, and, finally and dramatically, the Open Admission experiment at the City University of New York.

The work at CUNY has directly or indirectly influenced curriculum and pedagogy elsewhere. All of us in higher education are to one extent or another dealing with new students, of whom the Open Admission matriculants were only the most dramatically different examples. We can no longer depend on having students who, as children, gradually and imperceptibly learned procedures

7. John Henry Newman, *The Idea of a University* (1852; rpt. Westminster, Md.: Christian Classics, 1972), 177–78.

for conceptualization. And if we value those procedures for their capacity to formulate and convey complex, sophisticated thought, then we must learn to teach these academic processes to beginners. As Mina Shaughnessy says, we must stop "guarding the tower,"[8] because by doing so we rapidly transform newcomers to our enterprise into disaffected aliens.

Teaching Students How Scholars Behave

I am suggesting that we teach students the colleagueship we cherish. Students need help in learning to converse rather than compete. Students are too little accustomed to listening to each other or to reading each other's work with attention. Without actual conversation about one's work, a novice writer is at a particular disadvantage. The lonely beginner condemned to the linearity of ink on the blank page hears all the wrong voices. As he tries to imagine those absent strangers to whom he must write, he hears the voices of doubt and despair: "You don't belong here. This paper will show your smart English teacher how stupid you are. You never could write anyway." We want students to drown out those voices with other voices—voices that impersonate the missing readers. Nancy Sommers's research in revision makes clear that experienced writers know how to imagine a reader who is "partially a reflection of themselves and functions as a critical and productive collaborator—a collaborator who has yet to love their work."[9] Students need the actual experience of sharing work in progress if they are ever to internalize this essential dialogue. Experienced writers can imagine the frame of reference of readers other than themselves. And we can best teach our students this concept of otherness by encouraging a dialectic situation.

Collaborative learning does not imply coauthorship. In fact, as we well know, colleagueship leads to a greater sense of authority and individual responsibility for one's work. When we share our work with colleagues, we proudly acknowledge their help, not simply to repay an honest debt, but to connect ourselves to the community of those who have helped us. We identify the context

8. Mina Shaughnessy, "Diving In," *College Composition and Communication* 27 (October 1976): 234–39.

9. Nancy Sommers, "Revision Strategies of Student Writers and Experienced Adult Writers," *College Composition and Communication* 31 (December 1980): 385.

in which we have been working by noting the people we have talked to about our work in progress. We also say, in effect, "here is my contribution to our ongoing conversation."

We have learned the ritual of formal acknowledgment, a ritual we should share with our students. Students should read and then write pages of acknowledgment. They should note the conversations they have had on their work in progress. By doing so they learn two important rituals of the academic community: intellectual honesty and the free exchange of ideas.

If we want students to behave like scholars, we must provide positive models of how scholars behave. English instructors who share their own work in progress with students teach these novices a great deal about processes of academic development and the interdependence of the scholarly community. English instructors who read, assign, and discuss a wide range of genres, including of course the genre of literary analysis, demonstrate that it is possible for a liberally educated person to be quite literally conversant with forms of writing in a variety of disciplines. Highly verbal English instructors who recognize that some individuals see order in the world initially through numbers or shapes rather than words show a respect for forms of thought different from their own. That respect will be returned by the more open attitude of math majors and studio art majors toward the mastery of the written code.

Why should the English scholar and teacher have to assume so much responsibility as chief guide in the community of liberally educated people? I believe our discipline makes us especially equipped to understand otherness. As literary critics, we spend much of our time mapping fictional worlds, so that we can better understand the strangers who live there. As composition scholars, we have assumed the related task of mapping the universe of discourse. I am suggesting that we abandon the fiefdoms and guard towers we learned to inhabit early in our socialization process. If we do so, we will draw more accurate maps, and these maps will help our students and ourselves to become more confident explorers, beyond Seventh Avenue, beyond Chicago, to the fascinating and exotic communities across the sea.

8   Literacy and Orality in Our Times
Walter J. Ong, S.J.

Connections between the teaching of composition and the teaching of literature are not always easy to establish. We can presume that if they were someone would have done so long ago. But, as Winifred Horner has made clear in her introduction to this book, no one has made the connections very evident or very functional. One reason has been that we have needed to develop a deeper understanding of what writing is and what reading is. One of the ways to deepen our understanding afforded by recent scholarship is, paradoxically, the growing knowledge of what thought processes and verbalization patterns were and are in primary oral cultures—cultures totally unaffected by writing and residually oral cultures. Set against the thought processes and verbalization patterns of oral cultures, chirographic processes and verbalization patterns—that is, processes and patterns governed directly or indirectly by writing—stand out in high relief, and certain interrelations between writing and reading become especially telling.

Strangely enough, those interested in writing and reading processes, either from a practical or a theoretical point of view, including the many and often brilliant structuralist and phenomenological analysts of textuality, have done little to enlarge understanding of these processes by contrasting writing and reading processes in depth with oral and oral-aural processes. This is what I propose to do here: to review the orality in our long cultural past in order to bring an understanding of it to bear on the present literary and paraliterary situation.

Many people like to believe that today reading is on the wane. We have all heard the complaint that television is ruining the reading habits of children. This is a contrastive judgment: "ruining" implies that all the time today's children spend before

This paper is reprinted with some alteration from Father Ong's earlier article, "Literacy and Orality in Our Times," *ADE Bulletin* 58 (September 1978): 1–7.

television sets yesterday's children spent with books. The implication appears at the very least naive. It is in fact very difficult to compare the present state of reading and writing skills or activity with those of the past because past student populations do not match those of the present. A few generations ago there was no academic population with today's mix of family and cultural backgrounds, with the same assortment of entering abilities and disabilities, of skills and lack of skills, of desires and aims. Not long ago, America was largely rural. Now it is overwhelmingly urban or urbanized, even in rural areas, and educational expectations have correspondingly changed. Not long ago blacks were locked by law—illegal law—into a situation where even the most talented were denied upward mobility. And no one pointed a condemning finger at dropouts in any group because everyone took for granted that most boys and girls undergoing academic education dropped out—at least during college, if they had not succeeded in dropping out earlier.

Even more important, the aims of literacy in the past were not quite the same as now. The McGuffey *Readers,* often cited in "back to basics" literature and talk, had objectives quite different from those commonly advanced today. They were in tune with our times in the sense that they were remedial texts—designed to improve the defective elementary and secondary education that William Holmes McGuffey blamed for the poor reading performance of his college students.[1] But "poor performance" meant largely poor oratorical performance: The McGuffey *Eclectic Readers* (so called because they adroitly incorporated bits of often violently competing theories) introduced their readers to "sound-conscious" literature. "Reading" in McGuffey's world tended to mean training for public speaking and "elocution contests." In the process the McGuffey *Readers* doubtless helped train writers, for, as Joseph Collignon has recently pointed out, the ability to write is closely connected with the ability to hear in one's imagination what a written text would sound like when read aloud.[2] But the McGuffey *Readers'* immediate aim was more directly oral.

1. On the McGuffey *Readers* see Robert Wood Lynn, "Civil Catechetics in Mid-Victorian America: Some Notes about American Civil Religion, Past and Present," *Religious Education* 68 (1973): 5–27.
2. Joseph Collignon, "Why Leroy Can't Write," *College English* 39 (1978): 852–59.

McGuffey *Readers* touted in rotund periods heroic figures inherited from the old oral world. "Ceasar was merciful, Scipio was continent, Hannibal was patient; but it was reserved for Washington to blend them all in one, and, like the lovely masterpiece of the Grecian artist, to exhibit in one glow of associated beauty, the pride of every model, and the perfection of every artist." This typical selection, from Lyman Beecher's "The Memory of Our Fathers," appears in McGuffey's *Rhetorical Guide, or Fifth Reader* (1844), 291.

As in Shakespeare's day and throughout earlier history in the West, literacy was still thought of in nineteenth-century America as somehow serving the needs of oratory, for education in the classical tradition had never been education in the "three R's"— which come from postclassical, post-Renaissance schools training for commerce and domestic economy—but had been education for the oral performance of the man in public affairs. Little wonder that Charles Dickens's platform readings from his novels met with such wild success in McGuffey's *America*. Oratorical power and literary style tended to be almost synonymous. (The implications of this for the dynamics of Dickens's storytelling are little understood.)

But oratorical literacy was actually on the wane even in Dickens's day. The long-term history of the McGuffey *Readers* in fact registers the gradual demise of the tradition. Regularly revised between 1836 and 1920, the McGuffeys moved more and more from oratorical to silent reading. Writing was subtly winning out everywhere over the old rhetorical public-speaking ethos.

These reflections give some idea of the ways the oral and writing traditions have been interacting through not only our distant past but also our rather recent past. Throughout, scholars appear to have been quite unaware of the oral-literacy contrasts and of the gradual inroads of literacy upon orality. No one seems to have noticed as the teaching of rhetoric, which in its Greek original, *techne rhetorike,* means public speaking, imperceptibly became more and more, over the centuries, the teaching of writing. Earlier generations took their own residual orality for granted, so much so that they really had not even thought of orality explicitly as a state of culture or of consciousness.

I shall treat orality and literacy in two ways, first examining the ubiquitous and persistent problem of moving from oral expression to writing, and then briefly considering some special approaches we might take in teaching writing today because of the new, secondary orality that surrounds us on radio and television. In both instances my remarks are intended to be provocative rather than inclusive. There is no way to treat this protean subject inclusively.

Although its founding fathers were steeped in a still strong oral and oratorical tradition, the United States was founded in literacy, as Denis Brogan liked to point out from his vantage point in England. Written documents—the Declaration of Independence and the Constitution—are crucial to our feeling of national identity in a way unmatched in any other nation through history, so far as I know. Most Americans, even those who write miserably, are so stubbornly literate in principle as to believe that what makes a word a real word is not its meaningful use in vocal exchange but rather its presence on the pages of a dictionary. We are so literate in ideology that we think writing comes naturally. We have to remind ourselves from time to time that writing is completely and irremediably artificial and that what you find in a dictionary are not real words but coded marks for voicing real words, exteriorly or in imagination.

To point out that writing is artificial is not to deny that it is essential for the realization of human potential and for the evolution of consciousness itself. Writing is an absolute necessity for the analytically sequential, linear organization of thought such as goes, for example, into an encyclopedia article. Without writing, as I have undertaken to explain in *The Presence of the Word* and in *Interfaces of the Word,* the mind simply cannot engage in this sort of thinking, which is unknown to primary oral cultures, where thought is exquisitely elaborated, not in analytic linearity, but in formulary fashion, through "rhapsodizing"—that is, stitching together proverbs, antitheses, epithets, and other standard devices for developing a subject or theme that ancient Greek and later rhetoricians would catalog as "commonplaces" or *loci (topoi).* Without writing the mind cannot even generate concepts such as "history" or "analysis," just as without print, and the massive accumulation of detailed documented knowledge that print makes possible, the mind cannot generate portmanteau concepts such as "culture" or "civilization," not to mention "macroeconomics" or "polyethylene." The *New English Dictionary* entry for "civilization" notes Boswell's report of 23 March 1772 that Dr. Samuel Johnson would not permit the word "civilization" in his first *Dictionary*—it was too much of a neologism. Probably most of the words in our English lexicon today represent concepts that could not even be formed without writing and, often, without print.

In the world of the creative imagination, writing appears necessary to produce accounts of human life—that is, of what Aristotle calls "action"—that are closely plotted in the sense in which Greek drama is closely plotted, with a steady rise of complex action to climax, peripeteia or reversal, and subsequent falling action and denouement. Oral genres of much length treating human "action" are typically not tightly organized in this fashion but are loosely knit and episodic. Greek drama, which first provides such tight plotting in the West, is the first verbal genre in the West to be controlled entirely by writing: staged plays were oral renditions of written compositions. Similarly, print, an extension and intensification of the visualized word produced by writing, appears absolutely, and somewhat mysteriously, necessary to produce tightly plotted narrative about the in-close human life world that we find in novels, which are the products of the deep interiorization of print achieved in the Romantic Age.

All this is to say that writing, and to a degree print, is absolutely essential not just for distributing knowledge but for performing the central noetic operations that a high-technology culture takes for granted.

But, however crucial for man to arrive at his present state of consciousness, writing is still totally artificial, a technology consciously and reflectively contrived. In this it contrasts with oral speech. In any and all cultures, every human being who is not physiologically or psychologically impaired inevitably learns to speak. Speech wells up out of the unconscious, supported by unconsciously organized grammatical structures that even the most ardent structural and transformational grammarians now admit can never all surface entirely into consciousness. Speech is structured through the entire fabric of the human person. Writing depends on consciously contrived rules.

Moreover, it depends on absences—which amount to the same thing as artificiality. I want to write a book that will be read by hundreds of thousands of people. So, please, everyone leave the room. I have to be alone to communicate. Let us face the utter factitiousness and fictitiousness of such a situation, which can in no way be considered natural or even normal.

To move from the entirely natural oral world into this artificial world of writing is bewildering and terrifying. How do I deal with persons who are not present to me and who never will be? For, except in the case of personal letters or their equivalents, writers commonly know almost none of their putative readers.

A recent article by a friend and former student of mine, Thomas Farrell, nicely isolates two of the basic problems a person has to face in moving from orality into the world of writing.[3] Everyone who teaches writing knows the common symptoms: students make assertions that are totally unsupported by reasons, or they make a series of statements that lack connections. Farrell notes that such performance is not necessarily an intellectual deficiency, but may be only a chirographic deficiency. It is quite consistent with oral conversational situations. In conversation, if you omit reasons backing a statement and your hearer wants them, the normal response is to ask you for them, to challenge you. If the connections between the statements you make are not supplied by the concrete situation—which can supply connections of the most complex, multilevel sort, as students of ethnomethodology well know—your interlocutor can be expected to ask you to specify the connections. Generally speaking, in live oral communication the hearer will not need many "logical" connections, again because the concrete situation supplies a full context that makes articulation, and thus abstraction, at many points superfluous.

For the writer the situation is totally different. No one is there to supply a real communicational context, to ask anything. There is no full context other than the one the writer can project. The writer has to provide all the back-up or fill-in. In the case of creative writing, the writer has to anticipate how much detail readers are willing and able to settle for. For there is no absolute measure of how much detail you have to supply in writing about anything. In expository writing, the writer must consider all the different senses in which any statement can be interpreted and correspondingly clarify meaning, making sure to anticipate every objection that might be made and to cover it suitably. Every objection? Well, not quite. The situation is even worse than that. Select objections. The objections that the readers being addressed might think of. How is the writer to know what a particular group of imagined readers might think of? How do you imagine a group

3. Thomas J. Farrell, "Literacy, Basics, and All That Jazz," *College English* 38 (1977): 443–59.

of readers anyway? For one thing, you have to read, read, read.
There is no way to write unless you read, and read a lot. The
writer's audience is always a fiction, and you have no way of
fictionalizing your audience unless you know some of the options
for imagining audiences—how audiences have been and are fic-
tionalized.

The writer has also to anticipate all the connections needed by
a particular audience of readers. In fictional or other narrative
writing this is an exceedingly intricate and elusive business. In
expository writing it is difficult, too. The writer has to learn to
be "logical," to put matters together in a sequential, linear pattern
so that anyone who comes along—or any of the group of readers
he is projecting—can make complete sense of what is being written. There are no live persons facing the writer to clarify his
thinking by their reactions. There is no feedback. There are no
auditors to look pleased or puzzled. This is a desperate world, a
terrifying world, a lonely, unpeopled world, not at all the world
of natural oral-aural exchange.

Everyone who writes must move at some point or points in his
or her life from the world of oral exchange and thought processes
into the curiously estranged and yet fantastically productive world
of absent audiences that the writer deals with. Today, however,
the orality away from which the writer moves is of two sorts. One
kind, to use a terminology I have developed in *Rhetoric, Romance, and Technology,* is "primary orality," the pristine orality
of mankind untouched by writing or print that remains still more
or less operative in areas sheltered to a greater or lesser degree
from the full impact of literacy and that is vestigial in us all. The
noetic processes of primary orality, as we have seen, are formulaic
and rhapsodic rather than analytic. As in Homeric epic and to a
great extent in classical oratory, particularly of the more orotund
variety, this orality operates with the sort of commonplaces, formulary expressions, and clichés ordinarily despised by fully literate folk—for, without writing, an oral culture must maintain its
knowledge by repeating it. Writing and, even more effectively,
print store what is known outside the mind and downgrade repetitive styles. In lieu of more elaborate analytic categories, primary oral culture also tends to break down issues into simple
polarities in terms of good and evil, "good guys" and "bad guys."

The other kind of orality we now live with I have called "secondary orality." This is the orality induced by radio and television,

and it is by no means independent of writing and print but is totally dependent on them. Without writing and print, electronic equipment cannot be manufactured, and radio and television programming cannot be managed. (It should be noted here that, despite its name, television is in a fundamental way an oral-aural medium. It must have sound and, so far as I know, never uses purely visual devices: the weather map you read without difficulty in the newspaper becomes a talk show on television, presided over by an articulate and attractive woman or an equally articulate and handsome man.)

The highly oral culture of our black urban ghettos as well as of certain isolated black and white rural areas is basically a primary oral culture in many ways, though it is more or less modified by contact with secondary orality today. The orality of nonghetto urban populations generally and of suburbia generally, white and black, is basically secondary orality. As Farrell has made clear in the article cited earlier, the problems of moving students out of the two kinds of orality are not the same.

A real incident will illustrate the way primary orality can manifest itself. It was reported to me a few years ago by a graduate student in a seminar I taught at Saint Louis University. He himself was teaching a class composed almost entirely of black inner-city students in a community college. It was the time of the Cambodia crisis during the Nixon administration. "What do you think of Nixon's action in Cambodia?" the instructor asked. A hand was raised. "Well?" "I wouldn't vote for that turkey. He raised his own salary."

Such an answer will raise the hackles of many teachers, who can find no sense in it at all. They find it purely emotional, not at all "logical," irrelevant to the question, and in general a blatant example of nonthought. However, some kind of basic understanding of thought processes in primary oral culture shows how this sort of response, in such a culture, is perfectly fitting as well as thoroughly intelligent and human.

The question put by the instructor called for some kind of intensive political analysis. In a primary oral culture, intensive analysis is not practiced, and not even thought of. The student was from a culture preserving much of primary orality. He was unconcerned with analysis, yet he recognized that the question was a question. The instructor was getting at something. What could it be? That is to say, into what commonplaces or *loci* or *topoi* could the issue be resolved? How could it be found to reinforce what everybody knew about the deeper issues of life? Selfishness and my reaction to selfishness might be what was at stake. So let's give that a try. "I wouldn't vote for that turkey. He raised his own salary." The reply had the added advantage for a primary oral culture of couching the issue in polarized terms of good and evil. Was Nixon a good guy or a bad guy? Clearly, a bad guy.

Before we write off—and note the term "write off"—this response as naive at our present state of chirographic and typographic culture, let us reflect that, sensed in depth, the question, "Is Nixon a good guy or a bad guy" was very likely what the instructor was really getting at anyway. Cambodia was just an example illustrating the instructor's real concern. Aristotle has said—or written? the exact mix of orality and chirography in Aristotle's works remains uncertain—that in rhetoric, which is fundamentally the art of public speaking or oratory, the example is the equivalent of induction in formal logical operations. Rhetorical examples and logical induction both move from individual instances to generalizations. The highly oral student handled the instructor's query as a rhetorical example, as a concrete instance referring to something at a higher, more generalized level of abstraction. It is rather unlikely that he had read Aristotle, but he was experientially familiar with the terrain of rhetoric. Orality sometimes provides nonanalytic shortcuts into the depths of human issues.

Let us take a second example. A couple of years ago, as a senior member of our department of English, I visited the class of a graduate assistant who was teaching writing. In one of the chairs sat a young man who, as I found subsequently, was from the highly oral inner-city black ghetto. He was very attentive, trying hard. But he had no textbook with him, and it was immediately apparent that he did not feel at all disadvantaged by this—even though the class was engaged in an analytic discussion of a text in the book with a view to a coming writing assignment. The student did not even try to look at the textbooks of any of the students near him. But he was clearly earnest, trying. Trying what? To be "with it"—just as, in his *Preface to Plato*, Eric Havelock has shown that the Greek boys in Plato's time had been trying to be "with it" as they got their Homer by heart. In a primary oral culture, education consists in identification, participation, getting into the act, feeling affinity with a culture's heroes, getting "with it"—not in analysis at all. This is what this freshman student thought the class was all about.

Plato's remedy for an educational tradition that operated simply to enable students to "get with it," to empathize with key figures in a given culture, rather than to analyze, was drastic, as Havelock has shown: Plato simply prescribed excluding all poets from his ideal republic so that genuine analytic thinking could get under way. He saw no other means of achieving what he felt was needed: a noetic *metanoia* or conversion, a complete turning around in mental procedures—which we now know meant in effect a conversion from oral to chirographic thought. Forget empathy and face up to genuinely abstract questions: What makes a couch a couch? What is couchness?

In our literate culture, you can go too far with analysis, too. Reacting to the classroom situation I had observed, I was not at all inclined to throw out all the poets. But after class I did try to bring home to the graduate teaching assistant the terrible injustice being done if someone did not understand what this student's problem was and try to help him work through it. In my own experience, this is not an impossible thing at all. But you have to know where you are coming from.

Let us take a third example. Father Patrick Essien, an African diocesan priest of the diocese of Ikot-Ekpene, in South-East State in Nigeria, who has just finished a doctorate in educational administration at Saint Louis University, comes from a primary oral culture of a small village of Annang, a tribe of some half-million persons. In the curriculum vitae in his dissertation, which is about the present educational serviceability of proverbs, he proudly displays his oral credentials by noting explicitly that no one is sure of the date of his birth, then produces complementary credentials as an experienced literate by carefully calculating what the most likely date is. Father Essien's father, now deceased, was a chief. Among the Annang, as among other peoples, this meant he was also a judge. He used to sit in judgment over such things as property disputes: charges, for example, by a plaintiff that another was pasturing his cattle or planting his yams on the plaintiff's property. The judge-chief would listen to both sides of the case, take the matter under advisement for a while, then cite a saying or proverb, another proverb, perhaps a third and a fourth, and then deliver the verdict. Plaintiff and defendant would leave satisfied.

"But," Father Essien smiles, "you had better give voice to the proper proverbs or sayings. Otherwise you are in deep trouble, for if you do not cite the ones that apply to the given case no one who hears the judgment is satisfied." The law is lodged in the proverbs or sayings of Annang culture—or the law was, for Father Essien remarks sadly that it is getting harder and harder to find anyone with the skills that his father practiced so well. The law has become something written and does not work that way any-more. Inevitably, Father Essien's feelings are mixed, and ago-nizing. The Annang must move into writing, for its advantages are incontestable. But writing entails the loss of much that was good and true and beautiful in the old primary oral culture. You do what you can: Father Essien's dissertation will preserve some of the orality, but alas! only in writing.

A few months ago I was telling this story to another friend. "Sayings still work that way in the oral world of young children," he said. "Sayings settle disputes." He had taken some children on a rather long car ride a few days before, and there was a dispute when one tried to preempt a window seat for the whole time. "Turn about is fair play," my friend had said, and the dispute evaporated. The boy at the window yielded his seat. My friend noted the psychodynamics of the episode: the saying saved the youngster's face. He was moved out of place not because he was weaker or less worthy or unloved—considerations always urgent in the agonistically structured lifeworld of primary orality—but because "Turn about is fair play." This was something everybody knew, or should know, part of the common store of knowledge that a culture consists in. There is a deep humanity in the noetic processes of primary orality.

Settling a property dispute among adults, however, is a quite different matter from settling children's disputes. Not all have recognized this. Literates have had trouble understanding oral cultures precisely because in a highly literate culture experience of primary orality—or something close to primary orality—is likely to be limited to experience of the child's world. Hence persons from highly literate cultures have commonly been unable to react understandingly to adult, sophisticated levels of behavior in oral cultures but have tended to view the whole of "native"—that is, oral—populations as "childlike," including admirably adult men and women, middle aged and older, who often have coped with life more adroitly and more successfully than their literate critics.

This defensive, depreciatory interpretation of another culture by literates is itself curiously childlike. It has forced literary scholars consciously or unconsciously espousing it to go through incredible intellectual contortions to make out the *Iliad* and *Odyssey* to be basically texts composed in writing instead of transcriptions of essentially oral performance, because of the supposition that oral performance is not capable of the sophistication these works manifest. Thanks to the work of Parry and Lord and Havelock and their now numerous epigoni, we should be beyond this today. We should know something of the psychodynamics of primary oral cultures, of primary oral noetics—how the mind works when it cannot rely directly or indirectly on writing and on the thought patterns that writing alone can initiate.

Once we know something about the psychodynamics of the oral mind, we can recognize that primary orality, at least in residual form, is still a factor in the thought habits of many of those to whom we are called upon to teach writing. Such recognition does not automatically solve our problems, but at least it enables us to identify them better. Our students from oral or residually oral cultures come not from an unorganized world, but from a world that is differently organized, in ways that can now be at least partly understood.

What of those students who come from the world of secondary oral culture? Does the oral world of radio and television drive all its denizens back from literate culture to the primary oral noetic economy? Of course not. If it did, that would be the end of radio and television. There is nothing on radio or television, however oral, not subject to some—and most often to utterly massive— chirographic and typographic control, which enters into program design, scripts, advertising, contractual agreements, diction, sentence structure, and countless other details. Primary orality cannot cope with electronic media. I recall talking to radio and television producers in Dakar a few years ago and speculating with them about how it would be to have a television series run by a *griot,* the West African singer of tales, oral purveyor of genealogies, crier of praises and taunts, custodian of the *loci* of the culture. An individual performance by a *griot* could prove interesting, the Senegalese media people knew, but would have to be carefully supervised, for the new kind of orality had made a world utterly different from the *griot*'s world, using different techniques. There was no way for a *griot* to program a radio or television series.

But how about the audience? Does the oral world of radio and television reintroduce its viewers, as against its programmers or performers, to primary oral noetics? It appears not in any sophisticated way at all. Television viewers show no tendency, so far as I can discern, to organize their knowledge and express themselves the way the Nigerian villagers do in Chinua Achebe's novels. They have no such oral mastery of proverbial thinking at all. As I have noted in *Rhetoric, Romance, and Technology,* even relatively unsophisticated audiences in a high-technology culture feel they should scorn formulas or clichés as such, though they might not always succeed in avoiding them. Consequently, clichés addressed to audiences in a high-technology milieu tend to be accompanied by signals, verbal or other, that downgrade the clichés themselves. Archie Bunker's clichés are systematically debased by his malapropisms. The audience is encouraged and assisted to reject them and laugh at them. This is only some of the abundant evidence that popular culture is discernibly under the influence of literacy today, and at many levels, even in its relatively unsophisticated members.

Secondary orality, in other words, is to varying degrees literate. In fact a residual primary orality, literacy, and secondary orality are interacting vigorously with one another in confusing complex patterns in our secondarily oral world.

This situation does not automatically create sensitivity to literature or equip everyone with the ability to write well, but it can be made to work toward such goals. The world of secondary orality is a media-conscious world. In fact, this is the world that effectively brought about the discovery of the contrast between primary orality and literacy and ultimately the contrast between both and secondary orality. Milman Parry and Albert Lord discovered the orality of ancient Homeric Greece not simply by studying texts but largely through sound recordings of twentieth-century Yugoslavian epic singers.

Because we live in a media-conscious world, we can make students aware of what this chapter has attempted to sketch: what oral speech is and what writing is by contrast. This awareness can increase sensitivity to literature and to the problems of writing.

I am not suggesting more courses in "the media." But I am suggesting that both those who teach writing and those who teach literature can in their teaching make a productive issue of the contrasts between the noetic and psychological milieu of primary orality, that of writing and print, and that of secondary orality. Understanding these differences not in terms merely of slogans but circumstantially and in depth is itself a liberal education.

Perhaps I will be permitted to use another and final example from close to home. Last year, in a program at Saint Louis University on "Man, Technology, and Society," funded by the National Endowment for the Humanities, we managed to include a course called "Technology and the Creation of Literature," which had to do with writing as a technology and its effects in producing literature in the full sense of the word: verbal communication actually composed in writing. This is what we are teaching when we teach writing. We are not teaching how to transcribe oral performance—as someone, we don't know who and we don't know how, transcribed the Homeric tales from the oral world and made them artificially for the first time into fixed texts that henceforward had to be not retold but interpreted. We are teaching composing in writing, putting words together not with the help of a live and vocal interlocutor but with the help of an imagined audience and of something mute outside us. Like it or not, we are teaching a technology, for not only print, but also writing itself is a technology—a matter of tools outside us and seemingly foreign to us, which we nevertheless can interiorize and make human, transforming them and enhancing our own thinking and verbalizing activities in the process, much as a musician interiorizes the machine in the crook of his arm that we call a violin.

I had treated this sort of subject earlier in graduate courses, but the course on "Technology and the Creation of Literature" had to be an undergraduate course by stipulation of the NEH grant. Somewhat to my surprise, it worked magnificently for undergraduate students. Their reception of the course showed conclusively that media-sensitive students today are fascinated by carefully worked out contrasts between primary oral performance and writing, and between both these and secondary orality, and that they are liberated by understanding what these contrasts are. The course was a demanding one. Readings included, besides secondary sources, books of the *Iliad* and the *Odyssey, The Mwindo Epic* of the Nyanga people in eastern Zaire, parts of Genesis,

some Old Testament wisdom literature, Plato's *Crito, Everyman,*
selections from *The Faerie Queene* and *Paradise Lost,* O. Henry's
The Gift of the Magi, Poe's *The Gold Bug,* and James's *The
Aspern Papers*—the whole gamut from complete primary orality
(totally episodic—before the taping of *The Mwindo Epic* no one
of the Banyanga had ever put together all the Mwindo stories in
sequence) to all-pervasive literacy (the key to Poe's plotting in
The Gold Bug is the reconstitution of a text, and in *The Aspern
Papers* the whole character of James's always absent protagonist
lodges in his hidden writings, which finally go up in flames).

If undergraduate students can be sensitive to the differences
between literacy and orality this course explored, I suggest that
it would help our understanding and our teaching of the writing
craft for us to be sensitive to them, too.

9   Reading, Writing, and Cultural Literacy

E. D. Hirsch, Jr.

In this essay I shall focus on a neglected topic in the pedagogy of reading and writing, namely *content*. I don't mean to say that content is neglected as an abstract necessity in our pedagogical theories; I mean only that our theorists pay little attention to *particular* contents in the classroom. That seems perfectly natural. Reading and writing are *skills*, are they not? And a skill is something (is it not?) that once learned, can be applied to *any* content. That is the assumption upon which our reading and writing theories usually have been based. But, for reasons I shall mention, that assumption has led us so much to neglect particular contents that we have necessarily fallen short also in imparting the formal skills of reading and writing.

Some in this audience will sense that my present emphasis on content—on *what* we teach people to read and write—represents a reversal for me, a shift from, and even a contradiction of, some of the sentiments I expressed in *The Philosophy of Composition* in 1977. There my emphasis was strongly on the teaching of skills in writing—and, by extension, in reading. I argued that to teach writing was to impart habitual skills that could be transferred from one writing task to another. I urged teachers to avoid adulterating composition courses with such distracting contents as logic, poetry, fiction, or the history of rhetoric. I argued that composition was a practical subject in its own right—a transferable technique like stroking a tennis ball. Moreover, I suggested that all we needed to teach this skill effectively was still more research into the most efficient ways of teaching its various subskills. That was therefore the research program I advocated.

Why have I now changed my mind? I will tell that story briefly, in the expectation that my concrete experiences in large-scale reading and writing research might persuade others of the dangers of neglecting particular contents.

141

My research began with an assumption and a goal. My assumption was of course that reading and writing are transferable skills. My goal was to base the stylistic evaluation of writing on its actual reader effects. Thus, I reasoned, if a piece of writing was stylistically degraded in a certain way, its degree of badness would be reflected in the differential effects of the good and bad versions on two large groups of readers. I supposed that because reading and writing are skills, and because the reading skills of two large groups were matched, two things would happen. First, the two groups would read the same text the same way. Second, the two groups would exhibit the same differential effects when pairs of texts were stylistically degraded in the same way.[1] In short, if we calibrated the reading skills of our two groups, we could always find the same effects from the same stylistic degradations.

The first assumption turned out to be true—that two reader groups at a particular session would read the same text in the same way. But the second assumption proved false—that the same degree of stylistic degradation would always have the same differential effects on two similar groups. As matters turned out, if a paper topic was familiar to our readers, the effect of stylistic degradation was relatively big, but if the paper's topic was unfamiliar, the differential effect became small. Moreover, if our audiences were artificially made familiar with the topic, the original small effect became big. Another way of achieving that same disconcerting result was simply to present the text pairs to two university groups on one occasion and to two community college groups on another. To community college students, a supposedly familiar topic like Grant and Lee proved as unfamiliar as Hegelian metaphysics.[2]

Because of this unexpected result, we found, paradoxically, not that our readers were measuring the stylistic quality of our texts, but rather that our texts were measuring the cultural information

1. Stylistic degradation meant changing parallel constructions to non parallel ones and putting important ideas in the middle rather than at the beginnings or endings of sentences. It did not mean changing the original phrasing. Essentially, the versions were kept synonymous.

2. The reader cannot be expected from this short description to understand the details of the experiment. Fuller accounts can be found in David Harrington and E. D. Hirsch, Jr., "Measuring the Communicative Effectiveness of Prose," in *Writing,* ed. J. Domininc, C. Fredricksen, and N. Whiteman (Hillsdale, N.J.: Erlbaum Associates, 1981), and in E. D. Hirsch, Jr., "Culture and Literacy," *Journal of Basic Writing* 3, no. 1 (1981): 27–47.

of our readers. What had started out as a test of writing quality ended up as a test of cultural literacy. We therefore had to abandon our starting assumption that reading and writing are transferable, technical skills. We found, on the contrary, that it was not possible to separate reading skills from the particular cultural information our readers happened to possess. Of course, I don't expect my quick summary of these results to have quite the same disorienting effect on others as they had on me. Our experiments were conducted over many months with many audiences. Although we explored numerous ways of nullifying the effects of these cultural variables, we had not the slightest success. Only when such realities repeatedly hit one on the head do one's cherished ideas get changed.

Now, speaking as an ex-formalist, I believe I see clearly why pedagogical formalism had been the dominant assumption of reading and writing theory. Apart from its political attractions, which I'll mention later on, the great intellectual attraction of pedagogical formalism is the one that dazzled me when I was writing *The Philosophy of Composition*—it was the idea that we could teach people how to write in a short time by teaching them the underlying principles common to all writing tasks. Teach students, I thought, the forms and principles, and the contents will take care of themselves. That has been the dominant hope in the history of American educational theory. Let pupils learn such formal skills as how to think, how to read, how to write, and then let them apply these skills to the multifarious domains of life beyond the school. Quite naturally, this has also been the guiding idea of composition theory—through all its internal debates whether "process versus product," or "logic versus linguistics."

Our pedagogical emphasis on skill rather than on particular contents may now have gone so far that technique itself has begun to suffer. That is the view of our best researcher in the field of reading—Richard C. Anderson, who recently held a press conference on his findings, duly reported in the *Washington Post* of 30 November 1981 in a piece by William Raspberry.[3]

They're Teaching Too Much Reading

The reason our children are such poor readers is that we spend too much time teaching them [how] to read.

3. Copyright © 1982, The Washington Post Company, reprinted with permission.

That, at least, is the intriguing conclusion of an educator who has spent a lot of time looking at the problem of reading in the nation's public schools. And as contradictory as it sounds, he made a good case for his contention during a recent press conference at the Rayburn House Office Building.

The real problem, as reflected in standardized tests, national assessments of education and other measures of pupil achievement, is not the thing we normally think of when we talk about reading: learning to pronounce words and to understand their meanings. The problem is in reading *comprehension:* teaching children to think about what they read.

"National test scores show that American schools have been making steady progress in teaching young children the fundamentals of reading," Richard C. Anderson, director of the University of Illinois Center for the Study of Reading, said at the Nov. 16 conference. "However, scores are still poor in the middle and upper grades where more complex reading and thinking skills are required. We are now quite sure we know some fundamental reasons for poor performance. Careful analysis of reading programs has revealed that children are not being given enough help in learning to think about *what* they read. Too much classroom time is spent on workbook exercises that are irrelevant—and often counterproductive—to the goal of reading with comprehension," he said. . . . (No adult is interested in reading for the sake of reading, and there is no reason to suppose that children are any different—at least after the exhilaration of learning the basic skills. . . .) Anderson's seemingly paradoxical thesis may turn out to be altogether reasonable: the way to improve our children's reading is to spend a lot less time teaching them [how] to read.

One of the important findings in Anderson's more technical publications applies equally to both reading and writing, and this is his key point: What is written down or read typically takes for granted a great deal more information about the topic than the explicit surface features of language can possibly state.[4] Teaching that emphasizes the linguistic and rhetorical features of writing is thus inherently incomplete. The manipulation of technical features—including rhetorical, audience-oriented features, carries so much hidden, unspoken information that the linguistic and rhe-

4. See M. S. Steffensen, C. Joag-Des, and R. C. Anderson, "A Cross-Cultural Perspective on Reading Comprehension," *Reading Research Quarterly* 15, no. 1 (1979): 10–29.

torical features themselves are the smaller part of the transaction. The larger part is the silent, cultural dimension, which consists of brute information, not technique.

As a very brief example of my point, let me mention some of the current attitudes toward the enhancement of students' vocabulary. Ever since the heyday of generative grammar fifteen or twenty years ago, the most sophisticated view of writing pedagogy has been that vocabulary should be a minor element of instruction. As linguists say, vocabulary is "merely a lexical matter"—by which they mean something accidental to the permanent formal structure of language. But this view is incomplete. Anderson and others have shown that the conventions and vocabularies of writing constitute a subtext that cannot be detached from the text. The repeatable surface elements of language cannot be successfully separated from vast domains of underlying cultural information, and an essential aspect of that information is knowledge about the world contained in knowledge of words. Moreover, if we take vocabulary in its largest sense as a knowledge of all sorts of particular linguistic conventions, then this kind of brute information is an essential part of the repertory of language. Information is not detachable from linguistic structure.

What does this undetachability principle imply for our teaching? It means we cannot do a good job of teaching reading and writing if we neglect, by concentrating on technique, the *particular* cultural vocabularies we want to teach. To teach form alone is to perpetuate illiteracy even at the level of form. To teach reading and writing well, we can't reside comfortably in rhetorical expertise but must make difficult decisions about which *particular* cultural vocabularies we wish to impart to our students. And if that is so we will need to ask, Is there a central canon of cultural information that is analogous to the central canon of literature? Is there a *cultural* content that defines true literacy?

Just for a moment let us suppose that such a body of cultural information exists. And let us call its possession "cultural literacy." My argument is that you cannot have linguistic literacy without cultural literacy, that competence in reading or writing cannot go further than the cultural information that reading and writing presuppose. Hence cultural literacy is not just an abstraction but is a reality on which our success in teaching linguistic literacy depends.

But what in principle is cultural literacy? Can it be defined? Can it be consciously and explicitly sought? Let me suggest a purely structural definition: cultural literacy is that knowledge that enables a writer or reader to know what other writers and readers know within the literate culture. Thus it is not only a knowledge of convention and vocabularies but is also a knowledge *that* this information is widely shared by others. Moreover, since this shared culture is changing at its edges, the content of cultural literacy is also changing. New things become part of it and old things drop away—even while the more permanent central core remains. For instance, over the past few years, the term "DNA" has become part of cultural literacy. It is a word whose use requires not just our own vague information, but also a sense of the vague information we share with other literate people. A much older word in cultural literacy might be, for instance, "Shakespeare," while a less certain word in current literacy might be "Spenser."

I suppose we all have a vague sense of what cultural literacy is—of what is at its center and what is at its unstable periphery. But this vague sense is not enough. I think we cannot teach linguistic literacy well until we take explicit, political account of the concept of cultural literacy and make it an explicit goal of our teaching. That is a politically difficult move, of course—dangerous because it smacks of a ministry of culture. But to leave the matter entirely to individual teachers or institutions—without even offering them guidance or suggestions regarding particular cultural contents—is a neglect of our professional, even our technical, responsibility as teachers of literacy. Example: the curriculum guide to English teaching in high schools for the state of California offers not a single title of a single text as appropriate content for courses in reading and writing.

While that is a politically safe approach that avoids controversy as well as tyranny, it leaves the student open to the greater tyranny of one teacher's whim as well as the tyranny of ignorance. I believe that the Modern Language Association, National Council of Teachers of English, state councils on education, and the various national academies can hammer out compromises and specific goals for cultural literacy. At least they could try to do so, and nothing would be more useful in fostering technical reading and writing skills.

Besides participating in such an effort to define cultural literacy, our profession can also foster improvements in reading and writing by another sort of political act. We can encourage a more balanced union of form and content by resisting the drift toward making composition a separate empire of expertise. If Anderson and others are right, composition is *not* a special subject apart from its particular cultural contents. Writing conventions are *not* formal linguistic and rhetorical conventions but are changing elements of cultural knowledge. There is a technical, formal side to composition, of course, but its best application requires cultural, not technical goals. The role model for English teachers is still the great eighteenth-century professor of English Hugh Blair, who was called "professor of rhetoric *and* belles lettres." His task was the double one of teaching the technical skills of exposition as well as the cultural knowledge that is inseparable from those skills. He was professor of composition *and* literature. His great book on writing, which taught so many generations, was a book on both linguistic literacy *and* cultural literacy.

Illiteracy then, is not merely a deficiency in reading and writing skills. It is also a deficiency in cultural information. This double deficiency is best repaired in the traditional double way by a combination of literature *and* rhetoric, of linguistic form *and* cultural content. This is not to suggest that the job of teaching cultural literacy belongs to the English teacher alone. Of course not. Contributing to the broad knowledge that I have called "cultural literacy" is (or should be) a goal of all teaching in high schools and colleges. English teachers do have, though, a special, traditional responsibility for filling in the more egregious gaps in knowledge they find in their students. No other field is so close to living language as literature is, so close therefore to the cultural presuppositions of language. Fortunately for students, no other field is so vaguely conceived. No one has even managed to define "literature" as the word is actually used. Our strictly functional and aesthetic conception of literature is hardly more than a century old and can be easily swept aside in favor of a more serviceable concept bound up with general culture. Literacy is best conveyed by teachers who themselves exemplify—not just teach— a high degree of cultural literacy: by composition teachers who are literate, and by literature teachers who are experts in composition. The inherent doubleness of writing—of linguistic form and cultural content—requires an answering doubleness in ourselves.

10   Literacy, Art, and Politics in Departments of English

David S. Kaufer and Richard E. Young

What is the crucial gap to be bridged? It is not the "gap" (if that is the precise term) between traditional programs in literature and composition. The differences in professional status, quality of scholarship, and rewards of people working in these programs are well established, well known, and by and large accepted by faculties in English departments. This gap is less a rift than an acknowledged and accepted discrepancy. Composition programs are staffed by members of the literature faculty who agree to teach composition in return for the opportunity to teach also what they want and were trained to teach; or they are staffed by student acolytes who expect one day to become professors of literature. Even the most unpleasant and unrewarding activities can be accepted if they are intermittent or if there is reason to believe they will not continue indefinitely.[1]

Nor is the crucial gap that very real and disturbing rift between the values and beliefs of traditional literature faculties and those of the so-called New Rhetoricians, a group whose numbers and influence are increasing in departments of English. This heterogeneous group can be characterized by a scholarly commitment not to traditional composition but to a much more expansive

1. Part-time teachers should be mentioned here since many composition programs depend on them for their viability. Although part-timers are participants in the operation of the system, they are not members of it, having neither status nor influence in English departments. Their extensive use in composition programs is symptomatic of the low esteem in which composition programs are held. While the picture of department practices we sketch here is not likely to be challenged as inaccurate, it is worth pointing out that surveys over the past twenty years support it and reveal a remarkable stability in departmental practices on the teaching of composition; only recently have there been some signs of change. See, for example, Albert R. Kitzhaber, *Themes, Theories, and Therapy: The Teaching of Writing in College* (New York: McGraw-Hill, 1963); Thomas W. Wilcox, *The Anatomy of College English* (San Francisco: Jossey-Bass, 1973); Claude Gibson, "Business as Usual: Write, Write, Write," *CEA Forum* 9, no. 1 (1978): 3–9.

conception of rhetoric.[2] With this commitment has come an effort to reintroduce rhetoric into English studies as a serious academic discipline; and with this effort have come the disturbing disagreements over the proper definition of English studies, over the theory and pedagogy of composing and comprehending, over the makeup of faculties and the design of curricula, and over policies on salary, promotion, and retention.

But as important as this rift is, it is not, we believe, the crucial one. As we see it, the crucial gap to be bridged is the growing discrepancy between what English departments are equipped to deliver and what the rest of the academic community and society at large expect them to deliver. If English departments lose their present status and influence or if they disintegrate altogether, it is less likely to be from our internecine conflicts than from our having soured society's expectations about how we are to serve them.

Although English departments have been charged with the responsibility for the literacy of the society—for teaching reading and writing and for training teachers of reading and writing—we have failed to meet our responsibility.[3] We have simply not equipped ourselves to meet such large-scale educational and social needs. Most English departments continue to regard composition—the part of our work in which problems of literacy are addressed most directly—as a service rather than a discipline. Many, perhaps most, departments continue to maintain a system of rewards and punishments that discourages serious commitment to composition research and teaching. And they continue to assign instruction in composition to untrained teachers.

If this is the crucial gap (the gap between what we as English faculty have to offer and what society expects us to provide), how do we bridge it? An obvious but deceptively simple answer is to take steps to upgrade that part of English studies directly

2. Two recent anthologies give some sense of the diversity of interests in the group as well as their common purpose: Aviva Freedman and Ian Pringle, eds., *Reinventing the Rhetorical Tradition* (Ottawa: Canadian Council of Teachers of English, (1980); James J. Murphy, *The Rhetorical Tradition and Modern Writing* (New York: Modern Language Association, 1982).

3. The emphasis in our argument is on writing, but what we have to say about writing applies to a large extent to reading, at least to reading as a process of comprehending the entire range of discourse types, which includes nonfictional as well as fictional discourse.

concerned with literacy; to put it another way, we can take steps to establish composition as a serious academic discipline. But suppose we were to change department policies on composition research and instruction as has been recently proposed by the Modern Language Association,[4] giving faculty the necessary professional incentives and training composition teachers better. Would this result in the desired changes? Probably not. All we are likely to achieve is a higher-grade service program, something that remains far from a discipline. Upgrading composition from a service to a discipline requires not only reallocating time and resources but also changing the way we think about composition—our assumptions and the sense of commitment we bring to composition theory, research, and pedagogy.

We have not so much ignored the problem of literacy as we have placed our intellectual priorities elsewhere. Understanding why seems a reasonable first step in addressing the problem seriously and in establishing composition as a substantial academic discipline. (Perhaps "reestablishing" is more precise, since for two thousand years rhetoric was at the center of the humanistic disciplines.) Until an adequate history of our devaluation of rhetoric is written, we will be limited to broad chronologies and speculative reconstruction. Since Winifred Horner offers a useful chronology of developments in the history of rhetoric, there is no need to recapitulate it here. However, we would like to add some observations of our own. We begin by pointing out a curious dualism in the way we have come to view composing and the teaching of composition.

Two quite different assumptions about the nature of composing have been widely held in English departments—often by the same person.[5] The assumptions have functioned as presuppositions in our thinking not only about scholarly and pedagogical work in composition but about curriculum design and professional advancement as well. The first assumption separates writing from thinking, treating writing as a relatively trivial craft concerned largely with the conventions and mechanics of good prose—with grammar, usage, spelling, diction, organization principles, and so

4. "Working Paper of the Commission on the Future of the Profession," *PMLA* 96 (1981), esp. 537.

5. For a brief discussion of these two assumptions, see Louis T. Milic, "Theories of Style and Their Implications for the Teaching of Composition," *College Composition and Communication* 16 (1965): 66–69, 126.

on—the sort of thing one finds in composition handbooks. The craft of writing, as defined here, is composed of those aspects of writing that are so limited in scope and so well defined that it is possible to develop rigid generalizations about them that can be applied in almost any writing task. "Writing" in this sense tends to become the editing of what has already been produced by less well specified means.

Composition courses that emphasize the forms and norms of standard edited English are a kind of halfway house between high-school and college English. They may be necessary for subsequent college work, they may improve the student's ability to produce acceptable prose, and they obviously demand a great deal of the teacher's time and energy, but as intellectual activities they demand little, certainly in comparison with what is demanded by traditional literary scholarship and teaching. It is this view of writing that has allowed English departments in good conscience to staff composition courses with literate but untrained teachers.

The second assumption is that writing and thinking are inseparable. When thought, style, and—some add—the man are seen as inseparable, the process of writing tends to become mysterious, and such elusive notions as genius, talent, natural gifts, unconscious cerebration, and imagination are posited as explanations for successful performance. The mysteries of composing are those aspects of the process that are so poorly defined that we have little idea of what might be done, directly at least, to improve students' writing ability. Writing considered in terms of this second assumption is an art. The sources of excellence are much less clear when writing is viewed as an art rather than a craft, as are the requisites for effective teaching and learning.

It is this second assumption that leads to the frequently heard statement that writing can be learned but not taught.[6] It also leads to a reliance on extensive practice innocent of rhetorical theory and on extensive reading as the two principal means for helping students cultivate writing ability. What cannot be taught directly can nevertheless be encouraged. Explicit instruction based on the first assumption develops skill in the mechanical features of writing, a kind of rite of passage to the indirect study of its more mysterious nature, which is usually carried on not in composition

6. See, for example, Roger Sale, *On Writing* (New York: Random House, 1970), esp. 15–58.

courses but in literature courses under the tutelage of professors of literature.

Faculties in which either or both of these assumptions are prevalent are likely to discourage colleagues and students who want to devote their primary effort to the study and teaching of writing. If all that can be studied and taught is a relatively simple and explicit craft, a knowledge of which is already widely disseminated in the society, then composition specialists, at least at the college level, cannot hope for professional recognition by their peers. If writing is an art of the sort described here, there is little to teach, nor is there much that lends itself to scholarly inquiry. A mystery is, after all, mysterious. It is easy to understand why generations of English teachers have shied away from a commitment to the study and teaching of writing. It appears to offer little of interest to the serious scholar and little basis for professional advancement.

Because the art/craft dualism has been so well entrenched in English departments for so long, alternative assumptions have by and large been overlooked. Much of the rumbling in English departments today stems from the repudiation of this dualism by many New Rhetoricians and their effort to introduce an alternative that challenges the numerous time-honored practices and policies that depend upon it. The alternative, what might be called a "competence theory" of art,[7] downplays without rejecting the distinction between gifted and ungifted and focuses instead on the distinction between novice and expert. It also repudiates the distinction between craft and art and substitutes a continuum of activities that includes not only those associated with the conventional notion of craft but those we would characterize as creative as well. It affirms that any activity along this continuum that is isolatable and recurrent across instances of the composing process is potentially teachable. And it affirms that the entire process of composing can be the subject of profitable research. With these changes comes the possibility of a new discipline, or the reemergence of an older discipline of rhetoric with its roots in classical rhetoric but substantially expanded and altered by recent theory and research.

7. For a discussion of this position, see Richard Young, "Concepts of Art and the Teaching of Writing," in Murphy, *Rhetorical Tradition*, 130–41, esp. 134–39.

A competence theory of art assumes that plans are a common feature of all activities in the process of composing.[8] All of us have plans for generating grammatical sentences, for editing, for solving problems, for posing questions, for adapting discourse to particular audiences, and so on. Some of the plans are part of our tacit knowledge and some are explicit, some are used consciously and some unconsciously, some are strategic and some technical, some are mechanically applied rules and some require special knowledge and skill to be used effectively. One category of plans, heuristics, is of special interest here.

Heuristics are explicit strategic and tactical plans for effective guessing.[9] Because their explicitness often leads people to confuse them with rule-governed procedures, it is necessary to dwell for a moment on the difference between the two. A rule-governed plan specifies a finite series of steps that can be carried out consciously and mechanically without the aid of intuition or special ability, and if properly carried out always yields a correct result— for example, the plan for producing accurate sums in simple addition problems. In contrast, a heuristic provides a series of questions or operations whose results are always provisional. Although explicit and more or less systematic, heuristic search is not wholly conscious or mechanical: intuition, relevant knowledge, and skill are also necessary for acceptable results. The topoi of Aristotelian rhetoric, Socratic dialectic, stasis in Roman rhetoric, Kenneth Burke's dramatistic method, and Francis Christensen's generative rhetoric of the sentence are familiar examples of heuristic plans.

Heuristics are one means by which we translate our rhetorical knowledge into rhetorical practice, knowledge of everything from such narrow-gauge issues as emphasis in sentences to broad issues like the structure of argument or the nature of problems. One important characteristic of heuristics is that they can be taught and used by anyone with normal intelligence, though there is likely to be substantial variation in the skill with which they are used and in the acceptability of the results. Heuristics may not enable

8. Young, "Concepts of Art," 134. For a theory of such plans, see George A. Miller, Eugene Galanter, and Karl H. Pribram, *Plans and the Structure of Behavior* (New York: Holt, Rinehart and Winston, 1960).

9. Young, "Concepts of Art," 135–39. For a more detailed discussion see D. N. Perkins, *The Mind's Best Work* (Cambridge: Harvard University Press, 1981), 190–219, 245–74.

one to write like Milton, but they can help one significantly improve the quality of thought and prose.

How do we know which writing skills can be taught by heuristics? There is no simple answer beyond the obvious: the skill must require more than a single context-invariant (i.e., mechanical) rule, but it must not be so complex that the teacher is unable to devise an effective heuristic for acquiring it. Our beliefs change about what skills can be controlled by rigid rules and what can be guided by heuristics. Skills we once thought were mechanical we now know require heuristic training. For example, although some teachers still present rules for using the passive voice ("avoid the passive"), we know that passives are appropriate in many contexts and that students can be taught their appropriate use through heuristic rules of thumb.

More interesting still are heuristics for developing skills generally thought to be dependent on genius (or talent, or intelligence, or personality), such as the isolation and formulation of problems at the inception of original inquiry, a skill most of us would see as essential to creative thinking but that can be substantially improved by the use of heuristics.[10] In the paragraphs that follow, we want to review an instance in which we developed a heuristic plan for teaching students fair ways to refute an opponent's position in argumentive writing. Clearly, this skill cannot be controlled by mechanical rules; most of us would say it is a matter of art. On the other hand, the more complex plans provided by standard texts on argument are also insufficient for improving their skill. Upon recognizing their insufficiency, one might be inclined to attribute the skill to a special gift or native intelligence. But we think we can make a case for why this option is wrong and why heuristics can be devised for improving performance in ethical refutation.

When responsible writers attempt to refute an opponent's position, they try to present it as fairly as they present their own, and for pragmatic as well as ethical reasons; penalties are likely to be imposed by readers if they think the argument is unfair. If the writer ignores the opponent's position, he leaves the reader in doubt about whether a significant controversy is being ad-

10. For a discussion of a heuristic for problem formulation and efforts to use it in teaching, see Richard E. Young and Frank M. Koen, *The Tagmemic Discovery Procedure: An Evaluation of Its Uses in the Teaching of Rhetoric*, NEH grant no. EO–5238–71–116 (Ann Arbor: University of Michigan, 1973). (ERIC: ED084517.)

dressed; if he does not demonstrate that he is sensitive to what is reasonable in the opponent's position, the reader may suspect that the opponent has been reduced to a straw man. In either case the reader may well become suspicious and defensive. On the other hand, if the writer does not show that his position is superior to the opponent's, he gives the reader no basis for preferring it.

Students find it exceedingly difficult to avoid these pitfalls. Often they omit the opponent's position altogether; or if forced to discuss it, they diminish its reasonableness more than they have to, or should. Their difficulty seems to have little to do with their ability to evaluate evidence or fallacies—the ability that texts on argument seek to develop; students trained in these evaluation procedures still repeat the mistakes we have noted. In important controversies, both sides usually offer strong evidence and nonfallacious reasoning; in such cases even students who are capable of discriminating between strong and weak arguments find themselves in the unwelcome position of having to suppress or distort the opponent's position to make their case.

If conventional training in using evidence and avoiding fallacies cannot improve students' skill, what can? We believe that the ability to develop fair-minded refutations can be improved by heuristics. Socratic ironists, for example, appear to have a plan that enables them to refute a position by pretending to praise it. We found someone considered skilled in Socratic dialectic and asked him to produce a "thinking out loud" protocol—a procedure in which he was asked to compose while verbalizing his thoughts into a tape recorder.[11] (Such protocols can be a rich source of information for discovering heuristics operating in expert performance.) For his task, our expert was asked to refute arguments for affirmative action programs, an issue about which he was knowledgeable, while writing ironically as a rational advocate of affirmative action.

The protocol revealed his use of a simple plan. First, he searched the opponent's arguments for their crucial underlying assumptions. Then he tried to think of important contexts in which these assumptions do not consistently apply or apply only with unforeseen and undesirable consequences. Having located these contexts, he developed ironic statements praising the opponent's

11. For a detailed discussion of this project, see David S. Kaufer and Christine M. Neuwirth, "The Irony Game: Assessing a Writer's Adaptation to an Opponent," *Journal of Advanced Composition* 2 (1982): 89–101.

arguments for handling or clarifying these problematic situations. For example, he reasoned that a central argument supporting affirmative action hinged on the premise that affirmative action laws specify only goals rather than quotas for hiring. He further reasoned that this premise depends on the very general principle that any program that has desirable social goals and is voluntary is a good program. He then developed statements praising this principle in the context of cases where administrators were pressured to account for their failure to meet their goals.

To see if our expert's heuristic for ironic refutation could be taught, we designed an exercise that encouraged students to reproduce the process. We assembled a set of twenty-eight argumentative paragraphs with the following instructions: "pick out the general assumptions on which each argument seems to depend; then think of contexts where the assumptions do not apply even though the writer would probably want them to." Although we have not done a full-scale evaluation of the worth of the exercise, we do have encouraging preliminary results. The students who used the exercise before writing their arguments showed clear improvement in the way they reasoned. For example, one student writing against gun-control laws reasoned that gun-control advocates based some of their arguments on the assumption that keeping guns out of the hands of private citizens would save their lives. He also noted that this assumption is problematic where a criminal intruder intends to kill his victim. This insight gave the writer a basis for arguing against the opposing position without misrepresenting or suppressing it.

We have sought to offer here a partial explanation of why the problem of literacy has not been an issue of greater concern in departments of English and why English faculties have not been alive to theoretical assumptions that would enable them to acknowledge and address this problem. Despite appearances, English departments have not been guilty of a willful neglect of their responsibilities. Conventional policies and practices affecting the study and teaching of composition are driven at least in part by reasonable beliefs about the nature of art and composing, not by a deliberate disregard of the public interest or a selfish regard for our own desires.

But it should also be apparent that the present factionalism in departments of English, provoked by the emergence of the New Rhetoric, is not likely to be easily dispelled. We are not likely to

achieve a sudden unity when we realize that we have often mis-
understood each other—when we realize that the goals of the
New Rhetoric are not incompatible with the traditional goals of
English departments, or that we all are sustained by a common
intellectual tradition, or that when a New Rhetorician uses terms
like "art" and "composition" he means something quite different
than what the specialist in literature means by them. Our divisions
are not rooted in definitions, though differences in definitions have
exacerbated the situation. Furthermore, sharing a common past
does not require sharing present beliefs: we are all well acquainted
with the history of heresies. And protestations about common
goals are unlikely to draw us together if we are dubious about the
New Rhetorician's strategy for teaching them. Better understanding does not necessarily increase harmony. The divisions have
deeper roots—in significant beliefs that we all are reluctant to
abandon or compromise and in the policies and practices growing
out of these beliefs that have given English departments their
character and shape. Even the MLA's effort to change policies
and practices, welcome as that is, is not likely to heal the divisions
unless their philosophic origins are simultaneously addressed.

It would be disingenuous for us not to express our support for
a competence theory of composing broadly articulated by many
of the New Rhetoricians and our opposition to those more conventional assumptions about composing that have discouraged its
serious study. We should point out, however, that a competence
theory does not necessarily rule out the more conventional theory
of art. Both are time-honored efforts[12] to account for processes
as yet poorly understood; there are plenty of reasons for modest
claims on the part of both camps and little justification at present
for rejecting one theory out of hand in favor of the other. Furthermore, one theory can help correct the other. For example, a
competence theory can give the literary scholar more specific
criteria to consider before presuming that a text is the product of
an unaccountable ability. In turn, such notions as natural gifts
and unconscious processes ought to make adherents of a competence theory hesitate to assume that every feature of composing
can or should be reduced to patterned and explainable behavior
and ought to encourage their awareness of what is unique in a
writer's work.

12. For a historical perspective, see Jacqueline de Romilly, *Magic and Rhetoric
in Ancient Greece* (Cambridge: Harvard University Press, 1975).

There are, then, reasons why a rapprochement is possible between adherents of these two theories of art. They are not reasons why a rapprochement is necessary. It is necessary only if we want English departments to continue to hold their present position and power in American education. Society, ignorant of our battles, expects English departments to cultivate a literate public. If we fail, others will assume the responsibility, as already has begun to happen; another new rhetoric is likely to emerge, but outside English departments and uninformed by the rich traditions we draw on.[13] The gap within departments of English and the gap between what we are qualified to do and are expected to do will disappear—but to the relief of no one.

13. For an instance of this trend, see Richard Lloyd-Jones, "Focus and Resolution," *ADE Bulletin,* no. 57 (1978), 8.

11 Composing Our Differences
The Case for Literary Readings

Frederick Crews

This essay, like some of its neighbors, originated as a talk presented to one of the three sessions established by Winifred Horner at the 1981 Modern Language Association convention in New York. The manifest content of those sessions differed, but their latent content was the same: an attempt at entente between composition specialists and literary critics over their shared concern with student writing. By comparing outlooks, we were taking perspective on ourselves: our backgrounds, our assumptions, our methods, our hopes and our problems, even our rivalries and our limitations of knowledge. My view was, and remains, that we ought to be frank about those rivalries and limitations if we expect to reason together about matters of policy. And this seemed especially true of the issue I would eventually address—whether the readings in freshman English courses should include works of imaginative literature.

No one should underestimate the profound and long-standing antagonism that writing specialists have felt toward "the literati," as they have been sarcastically named. If the latter remain largely unaware of it, that is because most of them have always taken as little notice of composition as possible. A literatus, indeed, is likely to realize that he is scorned only if he himself ventures into the realm of composition theory or advice. Then, to his injured astonishment, he finds that his pronouncements about writing are regarded not as the garnered wisdom of a meticulous teacher, but as snobbish and ill-informed dilettantism. At that moment he resembles an imperial explorer who, planting a flag at the edge of a seemingly empty continent, is notified by a hail of arrows that the place is already inhabited. If he does not immediately set sail for home, he may learn by and by that the natives have their own culture and are actually proud of it. When he tries to subdue them with the mystic incantation *MLA,* they reply defiantly, *CCCC.*

Ill feeling toward the literati can be readily explained by the peonlike status of composition programs within or beneath the

159

English departments of major universities. Priding themselves on their "pure research" and their rarefied philosophical concerns, those departments have looked with distaste on efforts to impart literacy to masses of students who will never be able to grasp a paradox or date a text. Literary professors have tolerated freshman composition chiefly because it has provided subsistence for their graduate students, whose minds are not supposed to become too preoccupied with the drudgery at hand. Thus it is hard for those professors even to take in the recent assertions by writing experts not just that composition matters, but that it has been acquiring a theoretical basis in psycholinguistic research that puts to shame the teacup-rattling squabbles of the aesthetes. The disoriented literatus must feel rather like Virginia Woolf when she dated the ominous modern age from 1910, at which time, she observed, one's servants began turning unruly.

But let me take up the plight of the critic who *has* always cared about student prose—there are many, after all—and who publishes what he thinks he knows about it. If his work is coolly received by composition people, more may be involved than a penalty for the past sins of his colleagues as a group. There is a high likelihood that his dicta will be drastically out of tune with what the professionals have been thinking. For, in the first place, it probably won't occur to him to read their work. His journals are not their journals, and at any rate hasn't he learned how to teach writing all by himself, through trial and error in the classroom?

No doubt—but that classroom is typically situated on a "better" campus. It has been filled with students who, judged against the national average, already know how to write tolerably well. That they don't write well enough to suit the fastidious professor determines his approach; he sees their problem as mental laziness, and he demands that they stop sounding like bureaucrats and sociologists. (Thus he communicates his social attitudes as well as his advice about trimming nominal constructions and embedded elements.) He does not yet know what the experts could have told him, had he only asked: that to write as badly as a sociologist, one must first be able to write considerably better than most American freshmen can.

The real problem, however, is not that the critic's prescriptions are inappropriate; it is that they are entirely editorial. Dealing on a daily basis with students who turn out passable written work, he takes it for granted that young writers already know what they want to say and must simply strive to get it across in a crisper and less clichéd manner.[1] Thus he unwittingly identifies himself to the composition establishment as a retrograde figure—a spokesman for a despised "current-traditional paradigm" that stresses only polished end products at the expense of invention. What does he offer on such genuinely fruitful topics as the recursiveness of elements in the composing process or the use of heuristic devices or generating a thesis? Silence. He is setting the clock back to 1950.

If I have here been drawing what the police call a composite sketch of the suspect, let no one suppose that my own features have been omitted. I too had the effrontery to produce a composition text without much acquaintance with theory and research in the field, and though my *Random House Handbook* was focused from its earliest edition (1974) on the pursuit of adequate theses, I too began by overrating what we can reasonably expect a freshman writer to know and do.

Ironically, that misjudgment probably accounted for some of the book's original appeal. Whatever its defects, the first *Handbook* came across as a friendly, mildly irreverent statement from one would-be writer to others who found themselves confined by the artificial circumstances of a freshman composition course. My message—sometimes subliminal, sometimes explicit—was that writers are really on their own and that skepticism, not acquiescence to formulas, is the frame of mind most conducive to powerful exposition and argument. That was welcome news to some readers—namely, those who were already so adept and sophisticated that they needed only to trust writerly instincts that were already in place.

Luckily my book has survived into later editions that have profited from the counsel of veteran composition teachers. It is easy, now, to see why many readers found the first edition less than helpful in the classroom. On one side of an imaginary bound-

1. This is to say nothing of the newcomer to composition theory who assumes that his own literary-critical hobbyhorse provides him with a basis for judging the needs of student writers. If, for example, he is a votary of criticism that "decenters" or "deconstructs" literary meaning, he may even harbor reservations about the idea that a student paper should pursue a unitary thesis. For him, style is all: he exhorts freshmen raised on situation comedies and video games to pass beyond mere clarity, to cultivate the most esoteric tropes, and to rejoice in the subtlest resonances of a language whose plain denotations they do not yet control.

ary I had ranged "the rules"—those scholastic directives per-
petuated by and for punitive, error-obsessed wielders of red
pencils. On the other side stood a capacity for creating innovative,
risk-taking essays—a capacity that would somehow realize itself
as soon as the student was granted license to thumb his nose at
the fussbudgets. The trouble, of course, was that the minority of
students who possessed such a rhetorical gift didn't need my
exhortations, whereas the bewildered majority needed not ab-
solution from rules, but better rules. That is, they needed access
to the principles actually followed by practiced writers as they
tease their drafts toward a satisfactory final version. I have been
trying lately to supply those better rules—guidelines that might
enable even an ill-read and hesitant student to reduce the inci-
dence of error, combat choppiness and indistinctness in assertion,
exercise some stylistic options, and arrive at more complex and
defensible theses.

If there is a moral to this story, it is that critics who venture
into composition need all the help they can get from people whose
experience of freshman English is more extensive and more guided
by theory than their own. At the same time I am reluctant to say
that the viewpoint of an engaged amateur—whether as textbook
author or as instructor—is simply illegitimate. No one can say
for sure that writing is best taught through a sequence of tips and
exercises, even if the devices in question appear to have proved
their superiority to rival ones. For all we know, sheer engagement
counts for more than anything.

Let me pursue this point, for it will finally yield up what I have
to say about literary assignments. When we have exposed a class
to all the instruments that have been shown to offer short-term
benefits, do we have a group of writers before us? Instead we
may have experimental subjects who have provisionally mastered
several useful techniques but who still lack the integration of skills
that makes for permanent gains. We should not ignore the famous
Kitzhaber effect, whereby students' writing skills actually dete-
riorate in the course of a typical undergraduate career. If we are
aiming at something more than what the educationists barbarically
call "exit behaviors," we should at least consider the possibility
that the most effective component of our teaching may be neither
free writing nor sentence combining nor collaborative composing
nor peer criticism, but giving our students a close encounter with
shrewdly chosen readings.

To raise this possibility at all—and I do not mean to endorse it as a likelihood—is necessarily to take a less euphoric view of composition research than the one that now prevails in 4C's circles. The topics recently opened or deepened by such research are indeed full of promise, and the new emphasis on social-scientific criteria of experimental design has taken the field beyond its long era of naively anecdotal results. ("It worked for me last semester, so it must be the solution we have been waiting for.") But that same experimental ethos brings with it a temptation to overrate testable correlations whose significance for long-term stylistic competence may be dubious. Recall, for example, the hopes that were raised (and dashed) regarding "average length of T-unit" as a measure of "maturity." Or again, consider Don Hirsch's admirably candid second thoughts, expressed elsewhere in this volume, about "relative readability" as a variable that can be fairly isolated from a writer's total "cultural literacy." The truth is that we lack any measurable trait or combination of traits that can be confidently allowed to stand for facility with prose— and thus we also lack a basis for claiming that *the* best technique for teaching composition has been authoritatively identified.

People who regularly teach composition, as opposed to people who regularly do research, already know that their effectiveness is at best an approximate matter. There is no such thing as taking a heterogeneous group of edgy freshmen and "turning them all into writers" within an academic term or two. Improvement in composition, more perhaps than in any other skill, requires sustained motivation of a sort that teaching may or may not trigger. Individual students can be tutored and encouraged, whole classes may come to feel more at home with composing, but good results are always relative and often unaccountable. Whenever I begin to think otherwise, I recall my freshman student who, much to my delight, took a departmental prize—but she inconsiderately submitted the winning paper in the first week of the term, before I could even pretend to share the credit.

Conceivably, we could seize upon the prior history of such a student and use it as an opening gambit in justifying literary assignments. I happen to know that my prizewinner had already been exposed to a good deal of excellent literature and to none of the pedagogical innovations that have recently aroused so much hope in composition teachers. She thus resembled many eminent authors who have testified that literary reading produced strong effects on both their motivation and their style. We ourselves, furthermore, can remember the cathartic influence of certain works that we came to know in late adolescence. In the absence of better information on the issue, then, perhaps we should assign some literature in freshman English and hope that lightning will strike.

Unfortunately, this case is feeble on at least two counts. First, there are no grounds for singling out literary experience as the strongest component in producing fluency. The decisive factor might be sheer intelligence or the writing of frequent, carefully supervised essays in high school or the reading of worthy nonfiction or, most likely candidate of all, early and continuous habituation to educated speech in the home. The choice of literature amounts to special pleading. And, second, we would be utopians if we thought that a handful of poems and stories, sandwiched between lessons about the comma fault and the dangling modifier, would work miracles in altering of anyone's sensibility.

I nevertheless believe that an unsophistic justification for literary assignments can be made—not, however, at the expense of expository readings, whose pertinence for young writers is so obvious that nothing need be said about it. I am thinking only about adding or retaining a limited literary dimension. The case for literature must be modest, as befits a course in which only modest gains can usually be anticipated. Indeed, I think the best argument for imaginative works derives precisely from an understanding of the obstacles that sometimes make freshman English a disagreeable experience for all concerned.

Instructors tend to go stale on that course even if they are not required to teach too many sections at once, too many terms in a row. Why? The crushing workload of paper grading is only partly to blame; there is also the tedium of preaching the same precepts over and over to new phalanxes of recalcitrant learners. And, ironically, the more gimmicks the instructor adopts to elicit desired "behaviors," the worse the tedium becomes—for the chief bane of freshman English after a while is the scarcity of surprises it affords. To the degree that the instructor becomes a behavioral manipulator, his mind ceases to be engaged—and his students, easily sensing that fact, feel less like aspiring writers than like captives.

On their own side, students approach the course with misgivings about the instructor's notorious red pencil, which they expect to be wielded with harsh and arbitrary finickiness; about their want of anything to say on the paper topics that will be assigned; and about the ego threat posed by someone who is free to heap scorn on their beliefs in the guise of criticizing their prose. In all too many instances these fears are well grounded, for teachers who get no intellectual stimulation from a writing course may retreat to their political and social opinions. And when they do, the argumentative essays they have assigned cease to be occasions for learning and become weapons against insurrection. The student senses that he is expected not (as the teacher's rhetoric has it) to exercise his own judgment, but to kowtow to an approved line about gun control or abortion or offshore oil leases.

I am convinced that, on the level of departmental policy, the most promising remedy for such demoralization is to make room in the syllabus for first-rate literature. My reasons are practical to the point of banality. To begin with, instructors who are issued sections of freshman English tend to be literary types; if they are allowed to choose the works of literature they consider most engaging for both their students and themselves, they will surely be more alive in the classroom. In teaching literature, moreover, they needn't merely try, in a sporting spirit, to be open-minded, as they might have to do in the case of a two-valued public issue. They can readily entertain novel lines of interpretation that arise in papers and discussion. For literature, as Sidney told us, cannot be refuted since it nothing affirmeth, and even a critical monist knows that there are many avenues into meaning. An instructor who is also a good listener can come away from a partially "literary" composition course with a measure of eagerness to enter the fray again. (Needless to say, that effect would be nullified if the assigned works had no merit other than a reassuringly low "reading level" and a thematic appropriateness to the alleged interests of eighteen-year-olds.)

The combined immediacy and nonpropositionality of literature can be even more advantageous for students than for their instructor. Many freshmen, as we know, cherish their right to believe whatever they please, and much of the delicate and challenging work of freshman English consists of introducing them to community standards of evidence. Resistance to that work can express itself either in adamant dogmatism or, more commonly, in a reluctance to produce *any* idea for the instructor's scrutiny. Students often need to be coaxed into making an initial response from which a thesis could be developed. But even the wariest among them can find in literature a preformed world, full of images, stories, and enacted values that intersect their lives in any number of ways. A freshman whose brain turns to sludge when he is asked to write about world disarmament is likely to have a definite impression of a literary character. And though that impression may prove hard to support in a paper, the evidential problem will arise late enough so that it doesn't paralyze thought altogether.

This is not to deny that literary conventions pose difficulties of their own, or that some instructors notoriously teach critical theory instead of composition, or that an overbearing instructor can be just as bullying about poems as about essays. Yet a tactful instructor can use a poem, by virtue of its very opaqueness and multivalence, as a means of establishing a provisional authority more flexible and nondirective than his own. And in the potentially confrontational world of the freshman classroom that is a precious advantage, especially if the instructor has a knack for prompting lateral discussion. When students themselves begin trying to draw the line between allowable and illicit readings, the prospect of well-reasoned, cogently supported papers is no longer remote.

I have presented what I trust is a minimal, utilitarian, and therefore noninflammatory rationale for literary readings—namely, that a modicum of literature ought to combat the plague of sullenness that menaces every freshman English section. Nothing, you will notice, has been said about the capacity of literature to refine the young writer's ear or extend his range of sympathy or awaken his imagination or provide him with a quiver full of allusions and analogies. I happen to believe in those effects over the long term, but to speak about them avidly is to portray oneself as a soft head poised on a tweedy torso. Let it pass, for we have as yet no firm data on the ripening of imaginations.

Our focus in this volume falls on one course in which the requisite atmosphere for learning is constantly threatened by familiar pressures. Conceivably, that course is not even an optimum means for achieving its own modest ends. Perhaps composition should not be made a subject matter at all, but rather should be diffused through courses possessing their own intrinsic interest and their own well-delineated academic idiom. The point is at least worth debating. Meanwhile, however, we must do what we can to improve the morale and thereby the effectiveness of freshman English. Though we cannot say for certain what the makings of a writer are, we do know about the unmaking of many a composition class. If, as I believe, students and teachers alike can benefit from the open-endedness, the pleasure, and the stimulus to immediate reflection that literary readings can afford, then on this one point, at least, the interests of the literati and the composition professionals may coincide.

12 Literature and Composition
Allies or Rivals in the Classroom?

Edward P. J. Corbett

To ask whether literature and composition are allies or rivals in the classroom is to suggest that there is a potential for opposition between the two disciplines. For some English teachers even the suggestion that literature and composition might work at cross-purposes is scandalous; for others the suggestion is perfectly plausible. The majority of English teachers, however, might not want to respond to the question until such terms as *literature, composition,* and *classroom* are clarified. For them I can pose the issue more sharply by rephrasing the question in this way: Can expository writing be effectively taught in a composition classroom where the main or the only reading matter consists of such literary texts as poems, plays, short stories, and novels?

Whether there can be a fruitful symbiosis between literature and composition has become an issue in many English departments, because many of the tenured faculty who until recently taught literature courses exclusively are now having to teach composition to fill out their teaching loads. Although these teachers may regularly have assigned and evaluated writing in their literature classes, they ordinarily did not devote any classroom time to teaching their students how to write. They may have marked misspellings and solecisms and errors of fact and logic in their students' papers and have written lengthy general comments about the strengths and weaknesses of the papers, but they did not systematically instruct their students in the rhetoric of the kind of writing they assigned.

Now that these teachers are being asked to teach courses where the focus is supposed to be on teaching writing, many of them, understandably, are uncertain about how to teach writing on a rudimentary level. Many of them have not taught a freshman English class for fifteen or twenty years; some have never taught one as a full-time faculty member because, when they were hired as freshly minted Ph.D.s, assistant professors were so desperately needed to staff the heavily populated literature courses that they could not be spared to teach writing courses on any level. Since they have not been occupied in the teaching of writing, they have not kept up with—in fact, were probably unaware of—the exciting and enlightening research in rhetoric and composition that has been done in the past fifteen years or so. Saddled with the task of teaching a beginning-level writing course, they naturally tend to fall back on what they know best—literature. One can imagine the rationalizations that go on in their heads: "I can best teach my students how to write by making them pay close attention to how the masters of the language compose a text. My students can learn all kinds of valuable lessons about precise diction, about unusual sentence structures, about luminous figures of speech, about novel methods of organizing a text, and about human motivation by reading the classic poets, dramatists, and fiction writers."

There is ample precedent to justify this confidence that students can learn a skill like writing by simply observing the practice of experts. The ancient rhetoricians believed that a skill could be acquired by one or other or a combination of the following means: by precepts (*ars*), by practice (*exercitatio*), by imitation (*imitatio*).[1] Learning to write by reading the "best that is known and thought in the world" is essentially learning by imitation. A fundamental doctrine of the Sophistic school of rhetoric—best exemplified by Aristotle's contemporary Isocrates—was that the quickest and surest way to become skillful in oratory was to observe and imitate the master orators.[2] The motto of the Sophists might well have been "Do as I do, not as I say." When Augustine was a teacher of rhetoric before his conversion to Christianity, he taught his pupils primarily by dispensing precepts, but later he contended, in book 4 of his *De Doctrina Christiana,* that the best way to become an effective preacher of the word of God was to emulate the expert Christian preachers.[3]

1. See *Rhetorica ad Herennium,* trans. Harry Caplan (Cambridge: Harvard University Press, 1964), 1.2.3, pp. 7–9.

2. See chapter 3, "Sophistic Rhetoric," of George Kennedy's *Classical Rhetoric and Its Christian and Secular Tradition from Ancient to Modern Times* (Chapel Hill: University of North Carolina Press, 1980), 25–40.

3. "For those with acute and eager minds more readily learn eloquence by reading and hearing the eloquent than by following the rules of eloquence." Augustine, *De Doctrina Christiana,* trans. D. W. Robertson, Jr. (Indianapolis: Bobbs-Merrill, 1958), 4.3.4, p. 119.

The reason for the persistence of faith in the maxim that "good reading produces good writing" may be that a remarkable number of people who eventually became good writers feel that they learned to write from their repeated exposure to the products of accomplished writers. Many of them were omnivorous readers from early childhood on, and by the time they got to high school they had become so verbally adept just from all their reading that they were exempted from courses designed to teach students how to write. Many of the honors freshmen I taught over a period of ten years confessed to me that they had never had to take a writing course in their previous schooling. Whatever level of competence they had attained in handling the written medium they acquired largely by osmosis, from having steeped themselves in oceans of elegant prose. Many English teachers come from the ranks of those who were omnivorous readers and, having learned to write mainly through this process of osmosis, quite naturally believe that others too can learn to write by being exposed to great literature.

Historically, too, there is precedent for the view that literature and composition are mutually beneficial disciplines. By the very title he chose for the published version of the forty-seven lectures he delivered at the University of Edinburgh for twenty-four years, Hugh Blair indicated that he found literature and composition to be compatible disciplines—compatible enough that they belonged to the same classroom. He did not use the terms *literature* and *composition* in the title of his published lectures; instead, he used the terms that were fashionable in 1783, *rhetoric* and *belles lettres—Lectures on Rhetoric and Belles Lettres*. Blair was promoting the belletristic movement that two of his compatriots, Adam Smith and Henry Home, Lord Kames, had initiated about the middle of the eighteenth century. The reason these men felt that rhetoric and belles lettres—as well as some of the other arts, like painting, sculpture, architecture, and music—could be united under a common rubric is that all these arts shared a concern for such faculties as taste, judgment, imagination, and wit and such concepts as the sublime and the beautiful and the "pleasures of the imagination."

In his introductory lecture, Blair posited a double audience for the series of lectures that followed: those "employed in composition or in public speaking" and those who "may wish only to improve their taste with respect to writing and discourse and to acquire principles which will enable them to judge for themselves in that part of literature called Belles Lettres."[4] Some of the lectures, like the ten devoted to the rhetoric of the bar, the assembly, and the pulpit, were directed primarily to those of his students who wanted to become effective writers and speakers. Another group of lectures, the final thirteen, which dealt with various genres of literature, were clearly directed to those who wanted to become discriminating readers. Those lectures on belles lettres appealed to the same kind of audience of rising middle-class readers who were attracted by many of Joseph Addison's *Spectator* essays: those upwardly mobile citizens who were desperately seeking guidance in what to read and how to read.

But Blair did not view this dual audience as a disparate group. He firmly believed that would-be speakers and writers would become more skillful composers if they improved their skills in the reading of polite literature and that readers would become more discerning, more confident processors of literary texts if they understood something about how discourse in general was put together. He was perpetuating the tradition inherited from the two Roman rhetoricians he most admired, Cicero and Quintilian, both of whom had preached the value of a broad liberal education for those who wanted to succeed as public orators. Blair was enough of a humanist to recognize that the likeliest source of such a broad liberal education was not only the surviving literature of the Greeks and the Romans, but also the emerging literature of the British.

Hugh Blair was remarkably wide-ranging in the literature he recommended and discussed. He talks not only about the literary classics from a variety of cultures (the Greek, the Roman, the Hebrew, the Italian, the French, and the English), but also about a variety of genres (pastoral poetry, lyric poetry, didactic poetry, descriptive poetry, epic poetry, tragedy and comedy, historical writing, philosophical writing, epistolary writing, and even the newest form of belles lettres, the novel or, as he called it, "fictitious history"). In our time the province of literature, for many teachers of English, has shrunk to just English or American literature and sometimes to just one genre (the novel, for instance) of that national literature, and quite often to just the imaginative brands of discourse.

4. Hugh Blair, *Lectures on Rhetoric and Belles Lettres*, ed. Harold F. Harding (Carbondale: Southern Illinois University Press, 1965), 1:4–5.

Just as there is no internal or external evidence to indicate whether Blair's students had to submit any writing for evaluation in his course, so there is no evidence that they were required to read any of the literary texts he was discussing in his lectures. Since Blair's course at the University of Edinburgh regularly enrolled fifty to sixty students each time he offered it,[5] and since each of the forty-seven lectures in the series took at least an hour to deliver orally, I suspect there was not much interaction between lecturer and students in the classroom. The students were listeners rather than doers. If they were active at all in class, they were preoccupied with frantically inscribing as much of the lecture as they could get down in their notebooks.[6] One gets the impression, however, that students were expected to have read many of the classics that were discussed and that they were rigorously exercised in speaking and writing both in their preuniversity schooling and in their qualifying examinations. We must remember that at this time, when the educational standards at Oxford and Cambridge had slipped to a scandalously low level, the standards at all the Scottish universities were relentlessly exacting.

Unquestionably, Hugh Blair and his contemporaries such as Adam Smith, Lord Kames, George Campbell, Alexander Gerard, and David Hume established a model for much of the humanities education in nineteenth-century American colleges and universities. Blair's *Lectures on Rhetoric and Belles Lettres* and, to a lesser extent, George Campbell's *The Philosophy of Rhetoric* became staple textbooks in many of the schools, especially the ivy-league schools. Porter Perrin's and Albert Kitzhaber's doctoral dissertations on the history of rhetorical studies in American colleges in the eighteenth and nineteenth centuries confirm the shaping influence of these Scottish texts.[7] Ronald F. Reid's article on the history of the Boylston Professorship of Rhetoric and Oratory at Harvard and William Riley Parker's account of how English departments came into being in American universities in the last

5. Robert Morell Schmitz, *Hugh Blair* (Morningside Heights, N.Y.: King's Crown Press, 1948), 63.

6. Blair tells us in his introductory lecture that he was moved to publish his lectures because he knew that unauthorized copies of them were circulating in the student community.

7. Porter G. Perrin, "The Teaching of Rhetoric in the American Colleges before 1750," Ph.D. diss., University of Chicago, 1936; Albert R. Kitzhaber, "Rhetoric in American Colleges, 1850–1900," Ph.D. diss., University of Washington, 1953.

quarter of the nineteenth century supply additional details about the formation of the curricula in literature and composition.[8]

These historical studies make clear that English departments as we know them are of relatively recent origin and that American colleges and universities—as well as the Scottish universities—established their departments of English as much as a quarter of a century before either Oxford or Cambridge set up such a department. Harvard College, for instance, created its English department in 1876 as a way of retaining Francis James Child, who was being wooed by the newly founded Johns Hopkins University. Child had occupied Harvard's Boylston Professorship of Rhetoric and Oratory since 1851, but when he was a graduate student at a German university he developed a keen interest in early English linguistics, literature, and folklore—*philology* was the term used in those days for that area of study. So he was happy when his appointment as professor of English allowed him to turn his rhetoric classes over to his colleague John Richard Dennett and to spend his classroom time lecturing on Chaucer and Anglo-Saxon.

What happened at Harvard happened at most American colleges and universities established during the last quarter of the nineteenth century. If teachers of English investigate the early history of their colleges or universities, they will probably discover that the division now referred to as the Department of English originally bore a title like Department of Rhetoric and the English Language. The study of literature in that department had not yet been naturalized. But once literature was enfranchised, it quickly became a leading member of the establishment in the academy.

The newly enfranchised English departments, however, had a hard time defining their province. For a long time after their founding, they continued to teach speech, thus manifesting some allegiance to their roots in the study of rhetoric and oratory. But that concern for spoken eloquence rapidly waned in English departments, partly because English teachers wanted to dissociate themselves from the elocutionary movement that had come to dominate many of the speech programs and partly because a group of disaffected speech teachers broke away from the National

8. Ronald F. Reid, "The Boylston Professorship of Rhetoric and Oratory, 1806–1904: A Case Study of Changing Concepts of Rhetoric and Pedagogy," *Quarterly Journal of Speech* 45 (1959): 239–57; William Riley Parker, "Where Do English Departments Come From?" *College English* 28 (1967): 339–51.

Council of Teachers of English in 1915 and formed their own professional organization, known today as the Speech Communication Association.

But English departments did not have to search far to discover other tracts they could annex. There were not only those philological fiefdoms that German scholars had cultivated—the history of the language, the grammar of the language, the study of Anglo-Saxon and Middle English, the folk literature of a period or a region—but also the rich heritage of literature written in "modern" English. At first, little or no English literature written after the end of the seventeenth century gained entry into the curriculum, but gradually the literature of later and later periods was admitted. It would be interesting to discover just how far into the twentieth century it was before a piece of English literature written after 1900 was considered respectable enough to be admitted into the curriculum. The study of American literature on the scale that prevails today did not burgeon until after World War II when the veterans flooded back to the college campuses.

English teachers, however, were not content to restrict themselves to the canon of language and literature. Never having sharply defined their domain, yet being anxious to enhance their power and prestige within the university, English teachers began to assume responsibility for teaching courses in journalism, theater, great books, the Bible as literature, humanities, comparative literature, folklore, science fiction, the film and literature, the detective story, and so forth. There were countermoves, of course, to arrest the rampant imperialism of English departments. New departments were created, like Linguistics, Comparative Literature, American Studies, Folklore, to recover some of the territory that English had expropriated.

And all this while, English departments continued to teach the writing courses, not only the beginning course in composition but also upper-level courses in advanced composition, business English, technical writing, professional writing, and creative writing. Maintained almost as a sideline, these writing courses, especially the required freshman English course, ultimately made the English department the largest department in the typical American university and college.

As William Riley Parker pointed out in his article "Where Do English Departments Come From?" in *College English,* "Surprising as the idea may first appear to you, there was, of course, no compelling reason at the outset why the teaching of composition should have been entrusted to teachers of the English language and literature."[9] Training students in the art of spoken and written discourse traditionally belonged to teachers of rhetoric— and to all teachers, across the curriculum, in the Scottish universities. How did it happen that teachers of English language and literature won the contract to teach students how to write?

Professor Parker suggested that an accident of history accounts for English departments' becoming the custodians of the writing course. English departments began to emerge in American universities in the 1880s and the 1890s, just at a time, Parker says, when "the whole structure of higher education in America underwent profound changes, yielding to the pressures of new learning, the elective system, increased specialization, acceptance of the idea that practical and useful courses had a place in higher education, and, not least in importance, the actual doubling of college enrollments during the last quarter of the century" (348).

Wallace Douglas marks the beginning of that change at one of the flagship educational institutions in this country with Charles William Eliot's inaugural address as the new president of Harvard University on 19 October 1869.[10] The purport of Eliot's address was that Harvard would no longer be just a finishing school for the sons of the New England brahmins but that instead it would be, as Professor Douglas so aptly puts it, "a selection mechanism, a recruiting ground for new men for the apparatuses of state and industry, some of whom might even come to walk the corridors of power themselves" (132).

Harvard's lead was picked up by most of the private and public colleges existing at the time. The notion that higher education should provide students with the kind of broad liberal education that would enable them to assume leadership in society was not entirely abandoned, of course. But what was added to that notion was that higher education also had the obligation to train and to certify those who would become the clerks and the managers in the rapidly expanding world of business and industry.

9. Parker, "Where Do English Departments Come From?" 347.
10. Wallace Douglas, "Rhetoric for the Meritocracy: The Creation of Composition at Harvard," chapter 5 of Richard Ohmann's *English in America: A Radical View of the Profession* (New York: Oxford University Press, 1976), 97–132.

One of the roles English departments would play in that movement was to equip students with the verbal skills necessary for them to function efficiently as clerks and managers. Since English teachers traditionally dealt with the skillful use of language—mainly, of course, with its use for aesthetic purposes—administrators naturally thought of them as the proper custodians of this charge. Teachers of the Greek and Latin classics also traditionally dealt with the skillful use of language, but by the late nineteenth century the classics had declined considerably in enrollment and prestige on the college level; besides, those teachers dealt with "dead" languages. The teaching of such modern "live" languages as French, German, Spanish, and Italian had not yet caught on enough for those teachers to be seriously considered as the custodians of the writing course; besides, the future clerks and managers needed to know how to handle the English language, not those "foreign" languages.

Maybe the dismal history of the teaching of composition in America during the last quarter of the nineteenth century and about the first fifty years of the twentieth may be attributed largely to the fact that for most of that period English teachers were not disposed, either by their training or by their interest, to teach writing.[11] By the time the charge was thrust upon them to teach students how to write the kind of prose that keeps the wheels of business and industry spinning, the immensely rich rhetoric course that had been inherited from the Greek and Roman rhetors was being replaced with a curriculum that was concerned primarily with style or even more narrowly with "correct" grammar, punctuation, spelling, and usage. In seeking a replacement for the rich rhetorical tradition that was slipping away, the growing band of English teachers shifted their interest to linguistics and literature. Linguistics and literature are rich in their own ways, of course, and as English teachers became more knowledgeable about their native language and more sophisticated in their reading and analysis of literary texts, they were as absorbed in the pursuit of those disciplines as teachers of rhetoric had once been in the pursuit of theirs. Nevertheless, the composition course hung on in English departments and would not go away.

11. See Leonard Greenbaum's "The Tradition of Complaint," *College English* 31 (1969): 174–87 for an account of a number of proposals, over a period of about sixty years, to abolish or drastically alter the freshman course in English.

One of the persistent paradoxes about the composition course in American colleges and universities is that although it accounts for most of the size and budget of English departments, it has never been the prestige component in the curriculum. At most colleges and universities in America in the twentieth century, English departments have had to assign the largest portion of their staff and of their operating budget to teaching the freshman composition course. But the royal road to tenure in the department and to prestige in the profession ran not through the ghetto of the writing course but through the suburbs of the upper-division and graduate courses in language and literature. In her introduction, Winifred Horner has reminded us of the consequences of there being two "neighborhoods" in most English departments.

The disparities and inequities between those two neighborhoods were exacerbated by the booming enrollments in the schools for about twenty years after the end of World War II. There were more students than the schools could comfortably accommodate; there was a critical shortage of teachers; there was a seemingly inexhaustible supply of money available to the schools from state, federal, and foundation coffers. Because English departments occupied such a prominent position in the educational pecking order, they fared better than most other humanities departments in this atmosphere of general prosperity. They got an ever-increasing piece of the university budget because virtually every student who entered college had to take at least the freshman English course and very often had also to take a sophomore survey in literature. Heads of English departments went to the MLA convention every year at Christmastime hoping to hire, in that fiercely competitive seller's market, fresh Ph.D.s either to expand the already bulging staff of the department or to replace the stars who had been wooed away in the prevailing atmosphere of easy mobility.

But copia of any kind is not an unalloyed blessing. Obesity or flabbiness is always a danger in an environment of abundance. Because of the desperate need for teachers in those years, a lot of deadwood became permanently entrenched. Because of the flourishing teacher's market, graduate enrollments swelled, subsidized by teaching assistantships, which served two purposes: to attract the best graduate students from the available pool and to staff the inexorable freshman English program. Because of the booming enrollments in upper-division and graduate courses in those years, the senior members of the department got a chance to teach courses in their specialties every year, and before long they had staked out exclusive claims to many of the choice offerings of the department. Gradually the composition course was turned over entirely to teaching assistants and adjunct faculty, and as a result the regular faculty lost all contact with the freshman writing course.

The bubble burst about 1969. Not only did the supply of potential college students begin to shrink, but the nation's economy began to slow down. It is a commonplace that in such straitened times the humanities feel the pinch first. English departments did not feel the pinch as early and as drastically as some of the other departments in the humanities, but by the mid–1970s they too were crying "Ouch!" Because of the state of the economy, the diminished ranks of students began to gravitate toward those majors that could assure them jobs upon graduation. Enrollments in upper-division literature courses dwindled quickly and appreciably, but since students recognized that the ability to write was a marketable asset, enrollments in elective courses in writing substantially increased. Accordingly, many of those professors whose literature courses were canceled for lack of consumers had to fill out their teaching schedules with one or more writing courses.

It was at this point in the history of the rise and decline and threatened fall of English departments that the issue posed by my title came to a head. As I pointed out earlier, many of the senior professors who were drafted to teach composition courses pleaded that they could do an effective job of teaching writing if they were allowed to use literary texts as the stimulus and model for writing assignments. In other words, they were implying that literature and composition could be allies in the same classroom.

A number of cogent arguments can be advanced for a literature-based composition course. First of all, if vocationally minded students are foolish enough to want to avoid any exposure to courses in the humanities, getting them to read some literature in a writing course could be a subtle way of getting them "hooked on books," to use Dan Fader's phrase. Second, professors of English are usually more familiar and comfortable with literary texts than with the expository essays that serve as the stimulus and model for writing assignments in most freshman anthologies. Consequently, they can better analyze for their students how that kind of discourse has been put together, and they can talk much more enthusiastically about that kind of discourse than about the kind of prose that appears in the typical anthology of readings. As a matter of fact, even graduate students, who do most of the teaching of writing anyway, are better qualified by their training and their interest to talk about the poetics of a literary text than about the rhetoric of a piece of argumentative prose. Furthermore, ordinary students often enjoy reading literary texts—especially the narrative forms—more than the utilitarian forms of discourse. And maybe the strongest argument that the exponents of a literature-based composition course advance is that the best way to show students how to write is to expose them to the consummate artists in the handling of the language—the essayists, the dramatists, the fiction writers, and, above all, the poets.

Arguments like these are impressive and difficult to counter, but those who doubt the compatibility of literature and composition in the same classroom must be prepared to respond to them. One counterargument is that many English teachers have so narrowed their concept of what constitutes "literature" that the texts they choose for the composition course are often not apt or helpful models for the kind of writing students need to be exercised in. Exposure to a poem or a short story can teach students some valuable lessons about, for instance, precise, concrete, lively diction, and those lessons might have some carry-over value if a section of a paper they are writing requires a vivid description of a scene, a person, or an object. But that poem or that short story is not going to be a very helpful model for the student who has to write a book report for an economics class.

If teachers were as catholic as Hugh Blair in their view of what constitutes "literature," they might choose texts that were apt and helpful models for the kind of writing that should be done in a composition class. Excerpts from texts like David Hume's *Enquiry concerning Human Nature,* or Gilbert White's *The Natural History of Selborne,* or John Henry Newman's *The Idea of a University,* or Rachel Carson's *The Sea around Us* would provide more appropriate models for writing assignments in a composition course than the selections of imaginative literature that the proponents of literary texts commonly use for this purpose. But most teachers of literature do not know how to talk about the rhetorical dynamics of prose texts like those I named. And so they are more likely to use a text like Edgar Allan Poe's "The Fall of the House of Usher" than Poe's "The Philosophy of Composition."

In an article in which he advocated reform of the traditional English curriculum, John C. Gerber gave English teachers a new perspective on their mission by pointing out that they are basically teachers of reading and writing.[12] But as teachers of reading and writing they will not be very useful to their students, he said, unless they widen their purview of the texts worthy of consideration in their classrooms. They should be disposed to read and analyze texts that promote understanding as well as those that provide pleasure and stimulation. Gerber is equally catholic in his suggestions of the kinds of writing teachers should be prepared to engage their students in:

> By writing, I mean every type of written discourse, from the simplest sentence wrestled over in writing laboratories to the most subtle kind of imaginative work produced in our creative writing workshops. The term implies not only exposition but rhetoric, scientific and technical writing, business and professional writing, film and TV scenario writing, poetry and fiction writing, satire, and humor and burlesque, and whatever other modes are current and desired. (313)

For some of those kinds of writing, our favorite pieces of imaginative literature may not be as instructive as some quite pedestrian pieces of journalistic prose. The English teacher who feels comfortable only with belletristic texts is not likely to be a contented or even an effective teacher of the kind of reading and writing our students will have to deal with as citizens of the world.

Perhaps an even more telling counterargument stems from the seductive power of literature. Literature is so attractive to the typical English teacher and can be made so attractive to students that it often turns out to be a distraction from the main objective of a composition course, which is to teach students how to write the kind of utilitarian prose they will be asked to produce in their other college classes and later on in their jobs. The danger of a diversion increases when the teacher discovers that many of the students have to be taught how to read a literary text. The class then becomes primarily a workshop in how to read a poem—or a play or a novel or a short story. Before long the writing class has turned into a seminar in literary criticism.

12. John C. Gerber, "Suggestions for a Commonsense Reform of the English Curriculum," *College Composition and Communication* 28 (1977): 312–16.

Anyone who has served as a director of freshman English knows it requires constant vigilance to keep the teachers of the course on target, and if literary texts are admitted into the class the director's vigilance must be intensified. I spent more than twenty years of my professional career as a director of freshman English, first in a private university, where I had to supervise only 15–20 teachers of freshman English each year, including some teaching assistants, and then in a large state-supported university where I had to supervise 150–60 teachers of composition each year. In the private university where I taught, literary texts were not supposed to be used in the two-semester freshman composition course—mainly because all those who took the freshman English course were required to take two additional semesters of a survey course in either English literature or American literature during their sophomore year. It was fairly easy for me to monitor the teaching of that small band of instructors; but every year I would discover some of them—usually the new graduate teaching assistants—bootlegging literary texts into the course and, worst of all, focusing on those literary texts to the extent that the teaching of expository and argumentative writing was neglected for as much as three or four weeks of the semester.

I always understood why the young, eager instructors succumbed to the temptation to sneak literature into that writing class. Literature was what those instructors loved most and what their formal training had best qualified them to talk about. They yearned for an opportunity to introduce their students to the delights of literature. They were not deliberately ignoring the directives I had published for the course; they just could not resist the siren call of literature.

At the large state-supported university where I served as director of freshman English, all but about 5 percent of the freshmen had to take a three-quarter sequence in composition. The first-quarter course concentrated on expository writing; the second-quarter course concentrated on argumentative and persuasive writing; the third-quarter course was supposed to be devoted to further exercise in expository and argumentative writing based on the readings in a prescribed anthology of poems, plays, and short fiction. The syllabus for that third course, which I inherited with the job, made it very clear that the teachers were to engage the students in writing the same kinds of papers that were assigned during the first two quarters of the course and that they were not to be asked to write any kind of literary criticism of the texts.

As I look back upon that experience, I wonder whether it was fair or wise of us to dangle so much temptation before our instructors. For many of them this third-quarter course presented the only opportunity they had to teach literature as literature. Because of the large number of teachers involved in the freshman program, I am sure that many class periods were devoted to discussing literature as literature and that I never heard about most of those aberrations from the stated objectives of the course. But even without snooping about, I would find out about some of the defectors, and when I did I felt obliged to call them into my office and remind them of the directives in the syllabus.

I resorted to many positive efforts, of course, to keep the teachers on target. The syllabus, for instance, gave very specific instructions about how to discuss particular literary texts in class and about the kind of writing assignment that could be made after the discussion of those texts or similar ones. The training course that all new graduate teaching assistants had to take in the fall quarter gave explicit instructions about how to use the literary texts in teaching expository and argumentative writing. A lengthy handout entitled "A Composition Course Based upon Literature" that I prepared for my teachers I later incorporated into a collection of articles that Gary Tate and I published under the title *Teaching High School Composition* (New York: Oxford University Press, 1970). A brief quotation from that essay will illustrate the kind of assignment I felt was compatible with the objectives of the course:

> In order to write a paper on "Willy Loman's Failures as a Father," students would not have to operate as little literary critics, producing the kind of highly technical critical papers demanded of college-level English majors; they would have to respond to the literary text simply on a layman's level—on the same level that they would respond to an automobile accident that they had witnessed on the way home from school or to an account of that accident in the evening newspaper. Conceived of in this way, the course could be kept on target. And at the same time, students could have their valuable exposure to literature, and teachers could savor the delights of dealing with the kind of texts they feel most qualified to teach. (196)

My account of the struggle to keep a composition course on target could be echoed by any supervisor of a writing course, especially if the course is based on the reading of literary texts. The moral of all the tales would be that literary texts will more often than not serve as a distraction from, rather than a promoter of, the objectives of a writing course. Literature is important enough for the education of students that it deserves to be taught in a course all by itself. Writing can be demanded of students enrolled in the literature course, but the emphasis should be kept on the literature. Many of us have learned some valuable lessons about how to write from reading literature and having to write papers about it, but those valuable lessons represent incidental benefits from those activities. But a course designed primarily to teach writing is also an important part of our students' education, and as such it too deserves its own arena. Literature and composition should not have to compete in the same classroom.

My answer to the question posed by my title is beginning to emerge now. It may strike some readers as being an evasive yes-and-no answer, but I will try to make it as unequivocal as I can. As I suggested in the previous paragraph, literature and composition are fidgety rivals in the same classroom. They can be forced to coexist, but the effort needed to maintain that coerced association taxes the energy and strains the willpower of those who teach the course.

But to say that literature and composition should be relegated to separate classrooms is not to deny that they can be allies. They can, and do, complement one another. In 1958 a conference of prestigious teachers of English, meeting under the auspices of the American Studies Association, the College English Association, the Modern Language Association, and the National Council of Teachers of English, officially declared that the province of English consisted of three parts: language, literature, and composition.[13] Although those parts were regarded as autonomous, they were also regarded as coordinate and related. The recognition of that alliance was reinforced a few years later when the federal government funded the National Defense Education Act summer institutes for English teachers. Most of the more than one hundred institutes that were offered on college campuses each summer from 1965 to 1970 presented a program of three courses—one in

13. *Issues, Problems, and Approaches in the Teaching of English*, ed. George Winchester Stone, Jr. (New York: Holt, Rinehart, and Winston, 1961), 7.

language, one in literature, and one in composition. In those years the tripartite province of English showed that it could operate as a genuine federation.

The welfare of our profession is threatened by proposals to neglect any one of our constituencies or to make any one of them preeminent. Any loose talk about hostile camps developing within the federation must be regarded as treasonous. Although one or other of the constituencies of the province will inevitably attract more residents than the others, the hierarchy among the parts must never be determined by counting noses. In fact there is no need at all to establish a hierarchy. The three constituencies of our province would do well to adopt the slogan of Alexandre Dumas's Three Musketeers: "All for one, one for all—that is our device."